EXEGETICAL AND PRACTICAL
COMMENTARY ON ROMANS

Dr. J. P. McBeth

Exegetical and Practical Commentary on the Epistle to the Romans

By
J. P. McBETH, A.B., Th.M., Ph.D.

Fleming H. Revell Company
Old Tappan, New Jersey

J. P. McBeth, Ph.D.
Station A., Box 3985
Dallas, Texas

ISBN 0-8007-0724-9

Dr. L. R. Scarborough, Pres. Southwestern Baptist Theological Seminary, says:

"I regard it as one of the best interpretative commentaries that I have had the pleasure of studying. It shows careful study of the original language, high views of the practical application of the greatest of truths. He seems to have found the mind of Paul on some of the greatest subjects in all Biblical research. His English is chaste and glistens in the sunlight. His convictions are clear and deep and to me they run true to the mind of Paul, as he interpreted the mind of Christ. This commentary is a great polemic. He defends with Pauline clarity the most profound doctrines in this great work of Paul.

"Conservative scholarship has not been majoring in scholarly interpretation of God's Word in the last quarter of a century. There is great need for modern scholarship, whose feet are on the solid rock of Scriptural truth, whose head is cultured, profoundly scholarly, and whose heart is warm with the fire of a passionate evangelism, whose practical views of the application of the truth of Christianity are strong and steady, to go deep into the profoundities of truth and, in the light of modern scholarship and scientific investigation, give to the students of this age a reverent, interpretative view of God's Word."

FOREWORD

by L. R. SCARBOROUGH, A.B., D.D., LL.D.
President, Southwestern Baptist Theological Seminary

I have reviewed with great and encouraging interest the manuscript of this Commentary on Romans. Because of my appreciation of the author, my abiding valuation of Romans, and my supreme interest in the Apostle Paul, it gives me unusual pleasure to say a very heartful word concerning this book.

My first word is concerning the author. He is a young man. He is a well trained student, by graduation from a standard college—Hardin-Simmons University—and a Master's Degree with high standing from the Southwestern Baptist Theological Seminary. He came from a noble parentage. He says, "My mother is a theologian and my father had a philosophical mind." He was saved at fifteen, has been preaching since he was eighteen. He won high honors in college in the field of essay writing. He founded, through his church, a chair of Bible in a state school and was assistant teacher in that department, and has been giving diligent research for years and practical interpretation of God's Word to his people as a pastor. His preaching is Biblical, interpretative, and evangelistic. He is a scriptural soul-winner.

My second word is about this volume. I regard it as one of the best interpretative commentaries that I have had the pleasure of studying. It shows careful study of the original language, high views of the practical application of the greatest of truths. He seems to have found the mind of Paul on some of the greatest subjects in all Biblical research. His English is chaste and glistens in the sunlight. His convictions are clear and deep and to me they run true to the mind of Paul, as he interpreted the mind of Christ. This commentary is a great polemic.

He defends with Pauline clarity the most profound doctrines in this great work of Paul. The following illustration of what I mean is found in his discussion of a great doctrine in the eighth chapter. In referring to the substitutionary work of Jesus Christ, he writes:

"Not only was Christ our Substitute in death, but He Himself is our Substitute now and eternally. Therefore, Satan can never attack our souls. Everything, from the beginning of time through the death of Jesus to His eternal intercession, vividly manifests God as for the redeemed in substitution. We are saved by substitution. We are safe through substitution. As God substitutes Himself for the believer, then He can no more be against the believer than He could rebel against Himself. He could no more cast the Christian off than He could cast off Himself. To deny the Christian would be to deny Himself. To be against the Christian, He would have to be against Himself, and thereby He would cease to be God. Therefore, His existence is the guarantee of our existence. The impossibility of God's denial of Himself is our guarantee of the impossibility of His denying us. Not to be for the believer would be to oppose Himself. For the Substitute to be against the one whose place He took would be contrary to the nature of the Substitute, an impeachment of His character, and a division of His own nature. He would have to bring judgment against Himself before He could condemn the one for whom He is the Substitute. God being the Substitute, if there were any judgment, the Substitute must bear it; for the believer can not be touched since he has a Substitute and in that he has passed from condemnation into life. To condemn the one for whom He is the Substitute, God would have to rescind His own substitutionary action in the atonement. The death of Jesus can not be rescinded. That action is historical, and history can not be rescinded. The death of Jesus Christ is not only a historical fact, but Christ, in the mind of God, has stood 'a Lamb slain from the foundation of the world' (Rev. 13:8)— and eternity can not be rescinded. The heavens and the earth and all things therein were created for a redemptive purpose, and creation can not be rescinded. His substitutionary death could not be rescinded without rescinding the historical atonement, God's eternal purpose, His eternal will, even all eternity, and all creation. Substitution is according to His wisdom and purpose— His nature. Failure to regard His substitution would be the breakdown of His character, revolt in His own nature, and collapse of His immutability."

The above quotation is an illustration of the dynamic of this book.

My last word is the need of such literature as this book. Conservative scholarship has not been majoring in scholarly interpretation of God's Word in the last quarter of a century. There is great need for modern scholarship, whose feet are on the solid rock of Scriptural truth, whose head is cultured, profoundly scholarly, and whose heart is warm with the fire of a passionate evangelism, whose practical views of the application of the truth of Christianity are strong and steady, to go deep into the profundities of truth and, in the light of modern scholarship and scientific investigation, give to the students of this age a reverent, interpretative view of God's Word.

I could hope that this bright young author, and many another ambitious student of God's Word, would give themselves to a profound study and a scholarly interpretation of every book in the Bible. I cheer this author, commend his greatly interesting interpretation of Romans, and pray that God may bless him in further studies and bless multitudes of the lovers of Jesus Christ in the study of this challenging interpretation of the greatest of Paul's letters.

Fort Worth, Texas

This work of interpreting the Epistle of Romans from the Greek would never have been undertaken, except for the persistent encouragement from some of the best scholars among us. Even as I began it, I had no thought of it ever being published. I was doing it for my own benefit. As I would send excerpts of the exegesis to scholars over the land for criticism, they would urge me to offer it for publication. The manuscript received multiplied more commendation than I ever dreamed. Thus, I have been encouraged to offer the work to the religious public interested in theological restatement.

The book is not exhaustive. I was constantly mindful of its growing length, and purposed to keep within limits. The work is spiritual and practical rather than merely critical and philological. The author has been blessed with considerable sermon material from the study and exegesis.

I have had access to all the best commentaries on Romans. But my constant companion has been the Greek New Testament. For all points of exegesis, I have depended solely upon the Greek New Testament and the leadership of Him Who is THE TRUTH. I take no credit for the wonderful truths that may be found in this book—for God gave them to me, and I did not know them until He gave them to me.

I would here express my gratitude to Dr. W. F. Fry and to my faithful and talented wife for aiding in the reading of the manuscript and for helpful suggestions.

J.P.M.

CONTENTS

OUTLINE OF ROMANS

INTRODUCTION. 1:1-17.

    1. Salutation. 1:1-7.
    2. Thanksgiving and Desire. 1:8-15.
    3. The Thesis of the Epistle. 1:16-17.

DOCTRINAL. 1:18-8:39.

  1. The Doctrine of Sin. 1:18-3:20.

    (1) The Gentiles are condemned without the Law. 1:18-32.
    (2) The Jews are condemned with the Law. 2:1-29.
    (3) With or without the Law, all are condemned. 3:1-20.

  2. The Doctrine of Justification. 3:21-5:21.

    (1) Justification explained. 3:21-31.
    (2) Abraham was justified by faith. 4:1-25.
    (3) Justification by faith is the believer's assurance of final salvation. 5:1-11.
    (4) The grace of Christ transcends the offense of Adam. 5:12-21.

  3. The Doctrine of Sanctification. 6:1-8:39.

    (1) The believer's relation to sin. 6:1-7:6.
    (2) The believer's relation to law. 7:7-25.
    (3) The believer's relation to Christ. 8:1-39.

THE THEODICY. 9:1-11:36.

  1. The national rejection of Israel. 9:1-29.

    (1) Paul's heart is breaking over Israel's rejection. 9:1-5.
    (2) The principle of exclusion has co-existed all the time with selection. 9:6-13.
    (3) The exclusion is according to divine justice. 9:14-29.

  2. Israel alone is to blame for the rejection. 9:30-33.

    (1) The cause of Israel's rejection. 9:30-33.
    (2) Paul reassures them of his love by his grief. 10:1.
    (3) Faith-righteousness contrasted from law-righteousness. 10:2-13.
    (4) The Jews have had full opportunity to believe the gospel. 10:14-21.

3. The final restoration of Israel. 11:1-36.

(1) There is a remnant left in Israel. 11:1-10.
(2) The rejection of Israel is to issue in their restoration. 11:11-32.
(3) The doxology. 11:33-36.

PRACTICAL.   12:1-15:13.

1. The believer in spiritual relations. 12:1-2.
2. The believer in social relations. 12:3-21.
3. The believer in civic relations. 13:1-14.
4. The believer in moral relations. 14:1-15:13.

CONCLUSION.   15:14-16:27.

1. Reasons for the Epistle. 15:14-33.
2. Personal mention. 16:1-23.
3. Benediction. 16:25-27.

OUTLINE OF ROMANS

INTRODUCTION.   1:1-17.

DOCTRINAL.   1:18-8:39.

1. The Doctrine of Sin. 1:18-3:20.
2. The Doctrine of Justification. 3:21-5:21.
3. The Doctrine of Sanctification. 6:1-8:39.

THE THEODICY.   9:1-11:36.

1. The national rejection of Israel. 9:1-29.
2. Israel alone is to blame for the rejection. 9:30-10:21.
3. The final restoration of Israel. 11:1-36.

PRACTICAL.   12:1-15:13.

1. The believer in spiritual relations. 12:1-2.
2. The believer in social relations. 12:3-21.
3. The believer in civic relations. 13:1-14.
4. The believer in moral relations. 14:1-15:13.

CONCLUSION.   15:14-16:27.

INTRODUCTION
1 :1-17

1

INTRODUCTION

1:1-17

1. *Salutation.* 1:1-7

1:1

δοῦλος (servant) is an all inclusive term denoting in a general way Paul's relation of service to Christ. He gives a more particular duty in the term ἀπόστολος (apostle). δοῦλος Ἰησοῦ Χριστοῦ (servant of Jesus Christ) answers to the Hebrew עֶבֶד יְהוָה (servant of Jehovah). The name of Jesus Christ is substituted in the New Testament for Jehovah of the Old Testament.

δοῦλος (servant) must not be rendered "slave," for such translation would exclude the element of free will. The word means a "bondsman, or bondservant" (6:18). The Christian is a bondsman of his Lord. There are two essential Christian ideas in the word "bondservant": (1) the servant is purchased, (2) he is self-surrendered. Being purchased, the Christian feels an obligation to Christ, which can never be fully discharged. The new life develops through the sense of eternal debt to Christ. The thing that made Paul a missionary was that when he was saved, he felt a sense of debtorship to Christ and to the whole world (1:14)—a personal debt, one never to be forgotten —an infinite debt, one that could never be fully discharged. The second idea reveals the bondservant to be in perfect freedom of will. His surrender is not forced; it is self-surrender. He is self-surrendered because he has been purchased. It is the knowledge that we "have been bought with a price," that makes us cease to be our own and to live for Him who purchased us with His own blood.

A servant is not so much one who is "devoted to another to the disregard of one's own interest," as one who has made another's interest the all-including and determining factor in his own personal interests. A servant is not so much "one who gives himself up wholly to another's will," as one who wholly imbibes the will of another. Being a servant is not surrendering arms; it is taking up arms. It is not surrendering conviction; but executing a higher conviction which has become the very essence of one's being. No one will ever be a successful servant of Christ until God's will becomes his very own. Being a servant is not surrendering your will till you have no choice in the decision. Being a servant is having a will that chooses— not because of compulsion, nor expediency, nor because it is the will of the other; but because the will of the other is the nature of the servant. You are not a servant if you have no will in the execution of God's will; nor are you a servant if your will conflicts with His will; you are a servant if your will by nature is in accord with His holy will—which nature we obtain only in being born again (John 3:3).

κλητὸς ἀπόστολος (called apostle) is another idea prevalent in the Old Testament. The servant of the Old Testament became so by divine summons. Note Abraham (Gen. 12:1ff), Moses (Ex. 3:10), Isaiah (6:8f), Jeremiah (1:4f), etc. This expression should not be translated "called to be an apostle," but a "called apostle." "Called" is not a verb, but an adjective. This describes the origin and source of his apostleship. The term "called apostle" does not indicate a name nor a designation; it only denotes what kind of an apostle he is—one by divine and eternal summons.

κλητὸς (called) is without the article. The presence of the article would have denoted a specific call at a definite time. "Called to be an apostle" would indicate that the call was at a definite time, and would refer the apostleship indefinitely into the future. The absence of the article denotes a definite call at an indefinite time; and refers the call and office back with God in eternity. No point of time can be marked as the moment of Paul's call to apostleship. He has always been an apostle in the mind of God. There was never a time in all eternity when Paul was not an apostle.

"Called" is the one essential element in the qualification for apostleship. To be accepted as a "called apostle," the call had to be historically verified by a personal appointment from the Lord Jesus Christ (Luke 6:23; Acts 1:21f). This requirement, however, did not render Paul's apostleship questionable, though he was not in the original Twelve. Not only can he claim valid apostleship, but he could boast that he was not an ordinary apostle, for Christ made a special trip from heaven to earth to summon him personally unto apostleship (Acts 26:12-18). He is not an apostle by intrusion, nor by choice, nor by circumstance, nor even from the possession of such qualifications as would be fitting for the office, but like all other apostles, he was "called"; and that not only historically through a direct intervention of Christ, but through an eternal summons. The term "apostle" grew to embrace a wider meaning—including all those called by Christ without His personal intervention (cf. Acts 14:14; Romans 16:7; Gal. 1:19; 1 Cor. 12:28; Eph. 4:11). The absence of the article from ἀπόστολος (apostle) manifests Paul as having all the qualifications of any of the original apostles.

ἀφωρισμένος (having been separated, having been set apart, having been ordained, having been dedicated) is a passive perfect participle. When God acts in a perfect participle, His action is characterized by eternity. Therefore, the dedication of Paul has always been in the mind of God, and has stood as an eternal fact. This word gives a more definite description of κλητὸς (called). Paul has not only been called, but God ordained him in eternity to the gospel message of salvation. The dedication of Paul to the Gospel was preordained in God's eternal purpose

(Gal. 1:15f), revealed at his conversion (Acts 9:15; 26:16), and the divine purpose was historically fulfilled by the church at Antioch (Acts 13:2f). The presence, position, and relationship of Paul's name in this verse and to this word reveal that in all God's action with reference to Paul, God did not act independently of him. God dedicated him, and he dedicated himself. That is, Paul responded with the dedication of himself to God's eternal purpose. Paul's commission being preordained did not conflict with his freedom of will in acceptance. God's foreordination and man's freedom of will never conflict. Paul has used three significant terms here: δοῦλος (servant), κλητὸς (called), and ἀφωρισμένος (having been dedicated), all of which emphasises the sovereignty of God; and at the same time never interfering with the freedom of human choice.

εἰς εὐαγγέλιον θεοῦ (unto a divine gospel). εὐαγγέλιον (gospel) is not a verb, and therefore does not denote the work of preaching, nor the act of carrying the gospel. The word is a noun, and therefore denotes the message itself. The absence of the article denotes character, essence, and quality. θεοῦ (God), without the article, is best rendered deity or divine. Then the absence of the article from εὐαγγέλιον θεοῦ (divine gospel) denotes the gospel as having divine quality; that it is characterized by God himself; and is the very essence of God. The genitive θεοῦ (of God) also heightens the character of the gospel; denoting the gospel as both the possession of God and the essence of God. The latter idea is the more prominent here. Thus, the term is best rendered "divine gospel."

Paul being dedicated to the gospel, the carrying of the gospel follows naturally. Every one can not be personally dedicated to the active preaching of the gospel, but everyone can be personally dedicated to the gospel. When one is dedicated to the gospel, he will be dedicated to the active preaching of the gospel either personally or by proxy. If he preaches the gospel, surely his preaching is dedicated to the gospel. If another is in business, his business must be dedicated to the gospel. The farmer must not dedicate himself to his farming, but rather dedicate his farming to the gospel. The layman should not dedicate himself to his money, but his money to the gospel. Thus, all people, together with all their possessions, should be dedicated to the gospel; then it naturally follows that they are dedicated to the active preaching of the gospel either personally or by proxy. That is, those who do not preach, being dedicated to the gospel preached, will support the ministry.

Every person's life is dedicated to something; and that to which he is dedicated forms and molds his character. He that is dedicated to the world will become worldly. He that is dedicated to sin will become devilish. He that is dedicated to falsehood will become a liar. He that is dedicated to purity will become pure in heart and see God. He that is dedicated to God will become Christlike. Paul has dedicated himself, his all, to the one and only thing—the divine gospel. Man ought not to dedicate himself to anything to which God has not already dedicated him in eternity. Paul will not dedicate himself to another message, nor to another purpose, nor to another person. Being dedicated to a divine gospel, the apostle will not be shamed in life, nor in fruit, nor in reward in the hereafter.

1:2

ὃ προεπηγγείλατο, which He preannounced or promised beforehand, that is, before the promise was fulfilled. The gospel is not a new thing, neither is it a revision of the true religion. It is the fulfillment of the promise announced through His prophets. Paul read the fulfillment of the Old Covenant in the New Gospel. The gospel of Christ is the gospel of God come down to man. It is not a new gospel, but the heart of the Old. Beforehand, God's message was a promised Redeemer; now it is "Behold the Lamb of God, which taketh away the sin of the world" (John 1:29). This Messianic gospel is the fulfillment of

the hopes founded upon a divine promise.   The middle
voice denotes announcement upon authority.

διὰ τῶν προφητῶν αὐτοῦ ἐν γραφαῖς ἁγίαις (through His prophets in holy scriptures). The interpretation here is not to
be confined to the strict sense of the word; but refers to
Scripture as prophetic, rather than the prophets, or the
prophetical section of Scripture. The presence of the article with προφητῶν (prophets) denotes the unity of prophecy. The absence of the article from γραφαῖς (scriptures)
reveals the essence of Old Testament Scripture to be
prophetic; and therefore expresses the idea of prophecy,
rather than the men who prophesied. The absence of the
article further denotes the essence of all Old Testament
Scripture to be prophetic, rather than the prophetical
section alone. The Old Testament, as a whole, is prophetic of the New. The Law and the Psalms are prophetic
of Christ even as the prophetical section. The whole of
the Old Testament is one unified book of prophecy foretelling the promised Messiah. There is a scarlet thread
running through each Old Testament page, and becomes
in the New Testament the blood of Christ shed for the
ransom of many. Every Old Testament prophecy finds
its highest fulfillment, ultimate purpose, and end, in the
Christ of the New Testament.

The second verse identifies the divine gospel of the
first verse with the promised Son of the third verse. The
presence of the article with προφητῶν signfies that prophecy is a unity, and that all prophecy speaks with one voice
as to the promised Son. The absence of the article from
γραφαῖς further reveals the Son of prophecy to be the essence of Scripture; that is, Scripture is essentially prophetic, and the essence of prophecy is Messianic.

ἁγίαις (holy) emphasizes the divine character of the Old
Testament Scriptures as distinct from other writings.
The Old Testament is holy in that it contains the promises
of God Himself. The absence of the article denotes both
character and essence. This serves to heighten the em-

phasis of ἁγίαις (holy) in the description of the divine character of the Old Testament Scriptures.

1:3

περὶ τοῦ υἱοῦ αὐτοῦ (concerning His Son). God's Son, Jesus Christ, is the object to which the divine promise referred. Christ is the subject of the gospel of God. The presence of the article with υἱοῦ (Son) denotes personality. The gospel heads up in a Person—a living God.

Accepting the gospel is not subscribing to a book of dogmas, but the acceptance of a Person. Christianity is not a system of theology; it is a Person. Christianity is not a religion; it is a revelation. It is a revelation, not of a system of theology, but of a Person. Becoming a Christian is not living up to a new set of rules; but it is letting a New Person live in you, till it is no longer you that liveth, but Christ that liveth in you (cf. Gal. 2:20). Likewise, to refuse the gospel is to deny a Person. Unbelief is to disbelieve a Person. Sin is rebellion against a Person. Unbelief is transgression of heart against heart, rebellion of personality against personality, collision of natures. The sinner may disregard the message; but he is not dealing with the message merely, he is dealing with a Person. He may disregard the preacher's sermon, but it was a Person that was offered and not a sermon. Contempt of law does not do away with the law, but with the violator. Refusing the message does not bind the Person of the message, but the unbeliever. The message may be discarded, but the Person of the message forever sits on His throne. Casting off the message to the rubbish cannot dethrone the Person of the message, Who is the eternal King. The New Testament may be burned, but the Person of the New Testament can not be harmed; and He is the One "with which we have to do." Salvation is personal both with reference to the believer and to the One believed. The presence of the article with υἱοῦ (Son) places the emphasis of belief upon the Person, rather than upon the message. The Son is the essence of God's message, as is shown by the absence of the article from γραφαῖς ἁγίαις (holy scriptures). Christ is the embodiment of the divine Gospel. The divine Gospel and the divine Son are essentially the same. Christ is the gospel. The message is the articulated Christ. Therefore, the Father gives Himself to man in the Person of His son; the gospel message is the revelation of his offer to man; and belief in the Personal Christ is the moral response of the heart of man to the moral nature of the heart of God.

τοῦ γενομένου . . . (who was born of the seed of David, according to the flesh). The article with γενομένου (begotten, or born) identifies this birth as individual—the one birth—no other like it. Therefore, in His human lineage, He is a Son different to the sons. He is heir by birth to all that is common to the sons, yet individual in His birth—sinless, and God is His Father. He was born a man, but no other birth like His, nor any other man like Him.

According to the flesh, Jesus was a descendant of the great shepherd King of Israel, and therefore, a legal heir to His father David's throne. The Jews rightfully held this descent to be one of the sure prerequisites for the Messiah (Mark 12:35f; Heb. 7:14). The genealogy of Matthew (ch. 1) reveals Jesus as the Son of David by giving the lineage from Abraham to "Joseph, the husband of Mary, of whom was born Jesus, who is called Christ" (1:16). Luke (ch. 3) establishes the same relationship between Jesus and His father David; but traces the lineage the reverse order—going from Joseph, the foster-father of Jesus back to David, the son of Jesse. So well established were both the promise made to Abraham, and the lineage by which He came, that one of the common titles by which Jesus was known was the regal title "Son of David."

1:4

υἱοῦ θεοῦ (a divine Son). "According to the flesh" (verse 3) reveals Jesus, as a member of the human race, to be a descendant of David. Verse 4 states that Jesus has, in addition to His human nature, another nature, superior to His human nature—a divine nature. He did not get this nature from David. But being a divine Son (Ps. 2:7), Jesus has a divine Father, and therefore a divine nature. He is the Son of David; but above that, He is the Son of God. He will sit upon His father David's throne—and more, it shall be God's throne—God's eternal throne. Jesus preferred to refer to Himself as the Son of Man rather than as the Son of God. Yet Jesus was called the Son of God far more than He was ever called the Son of Man.

. . . ἐξ ἀναστάσεως νεκρῶν (Who was manifested with power (to be the) divine Son, according to the Spirit of holiness, by the resurrection from the dead). The lineal records establish beyond question who Jesus is according to His human nature. Now the resurrection of His body from the dead is a powerful declaration that Jesus, as to His divine nature, is the Son of God. The many previous claims made by Jesus (John 2:19; 10:18; 11:25; etc.) render His resurrection absolute proof of His divinity. The resurrection is both God's approval of Christ and divine vindication of Christ's claims. The divine Sonship of Jesus was declared by His Heavenly Father, as He accepted the relationship of Son (Ps. 2:7), at His baptism (Mark 1:10), at His transfiguration (Mark 9:7), then finally does God proclaim the divine Sonship of Jesus by His resurrection, which exhibits the relation in incontestable power.

ὁρίζω (manifest, declare, mark off, to place a marker, to set up a monument). This word means to mark off, to establish a boundary, to set up a landmark, to place a monument for permanent evidence of the established boundary of a territory. So Jesus' resurrection is a monument unto His deity. This is the proof that He is God. And His resurrection is not only evidence of His deity, but is a monument for perpetual evidence. This monument is not argumentative evidence. As one demonstration is worth a thousand arguments, so one monument reaching into heaven is worth all the arguments. A monument is conclusive evidence, by nature and virtue of what it is. It is not mute evidence but speaks without words. Likewise, the resurrection of Jesus as a monument unto His deity does not argue nor need to be argued, but is a divine declaration of His deity. The monument does not have to speak. No man can question His being God, in the light of the resurrection. This monument establishes beyond question all His claims.

Jesus lived with man as if He were God. He talked with the Father as though He were the divine Son. His life, His language, His foretelling of His Own resurrection (Matt. 12:38ff), and every relation to both man and the Heavenly Father were open claims unto deity. His resurrection established and set up an eternal monument unto all His claims. And this is not a little monument that only the taller people can see. No one needs to climb a tree as did Zacchaeus (Luke 19:4), for this glorious monument reaches even into the heavens so that it is evident unto "whosoever looketh."

The resurrection is the consummation of Christ's saving power (See the exegesis of 4:25). Thus, the resurrection of Jesus is a monument unto His saving power.

The noun ($\acute{o}\rho os$, a landmark, a marking stone—bearing inscriptions, stone slab, tablet set up on mortgaged property, to serve as a bond or register of the debt—cf. Liddell and Scott) was used of a monument raised on mortgaged property as evidence of its indebtedness and as security that the mortgaged property would be foreclosed in case of default in payment of debt. The monument was the initial evidence of final ownership in a foreclosure.

The resurrection of Jesus is a monument raised upon the territory of death—laying claim to the whole region of death—all those who died in Him. This monument is an immutable guarantee of the final triumph of life over death, and is an initial evidence of final ownership, and a foretaste of ultimate triumph. Though a man be dead, yet he shall live again: "He that believeth on me, though he die, yet shall he live" (John 11:25). Death can not pay the indebtedness on his territory, and the resurrection of Jesus is a monument signifying both initial and final ownership. By the authority of this monument, Jesus is going to foreclose on death one day, and the graves shall give up their dead in Christ, and He shall be the absolute owner and shall reign in life with eternal subjects, resurrected from the dead. Assurance, grace, and immutability are exhausted and consummated in the resurrection of Jesus, as a monument guaranteeing everything to the believer.

1:5

δι οὗ (through whom). This denotes the Lord as the agent in bestowing grace and appointing unto apostleship.

ἐλάβομεν (we received). The plural is most likely the editorial "we," which was in custom then even as now. Though Paul recognized that he is not the only one who can lay claims to this gift and calling; yet all indications are that he is speaking of himself, as this is in his salutation to his readers. He does not say he "obtained" grace, nor "worked" for it, but "received" the unmerited favor. Grace is shown even in this verb. A verb expressing any other means would be contradictory to grace. God provides the grace, then God gives the grace. Man's part is the reception of God's offered gift.

χάριν (grace). The root meaning of this word is unmerited favor. It was used to denote the favor of masters to their servants, and of the mercy of a superior in his gentleness toward an inferior. The New Testament writers convey in this word the only means of salvation, as they plead the righteousness of God for unrighteous men, pardon for the guilty, justification for the unjust, liberation for the bound, and eternal life for the dead. Grace pleads the merit of God for those who have no merit of their own. The accumulated merit of all generations is not enough to save the best soul that ever lived. The good they embodied and the virtue they possessed was not enough to render one soul meritorious before God, for the righteousness they had before God was not in excess to place God under obligation to them. They would have deserved no merit for having measured up to all they should have been; much less do they deserve merit for less than they should have been. "All sinned and fell short of the glory of God." (Rom. 3:23).

Grace cannot save the good, but the wicked. Grace can only save a sinner. Grace is for the person who deserves the full penalty of the law without mercy, and through grace the guilty receive the righteousness of God with all the glory and riches of heaven.

Adam and Eve both sinned. This was the whole race— the whole race was present in Adam, and in him the whole race fell. No man could save himself, for he was a servant of Satan, the dupe of sin, in the coil of the serpent, and in the jaws and power of death. Man fell as a race and therefore redemption was needed for the whole race. But no one could redeem himself, much less the race. To redeem the race, a member of the race must pay the penalty of the race in death. And in that death, the representative man must be righteous enough to be accepted of God as a holy sacrifice, and be able to suffer enough to pay the penalty. No man was able to be the Redeemer, for every man was under condemnation to die for his own sins. Only God was righteous enough for a sacrifice, and only He was able to suffer enough to pay the penalty. Not only was a penalty to be paid to make the unjust just before a just God (Rom. 3:26; 4:5), but that suffering must be efficacious in sacrifice to make the unrighteous righteous before a righteous God (2 Cor. 5:21). But God was not a member of the human race, while the Redeemer must be a member and a kinsman of the race redeemed. So in the wisdom of God, "the Word became flesh, and dwelt among us, and we beheld His glory, glory as of the only begotten from the Father, full of grace and truth" (John 1:14). Man was dead in his sins and trespasses, and could not redeem himself, much less atone for the whole race. So God became the brother of man in Jesus Christ, and on the cross Christ paid the penalty and made the sacrifice for the salvation of every one that believeth. His cross should have been ours; the shame He suffered was ours, and the death He died was not His own. He bore our iniquities, and we are just; He paid our penalty in death, whereby we have life, and "with his stripes we are healed" (Isa. 53:5). And he, who was dead, now lives by faith in Christ. Where man had nothing to pay, God made an appropriation for him. Man had no righteousness but God supplied it. Salvation is of the Lord—not of man but for the lost man. Salvation is so precious that whatever contributes to it, God chooses to place to His own account. Therefore, we are saved by grace, not as a means of salvation, but as the only means of salvation. Thus, we have the meaning of χάρις (grace).

καὶ ἀποστολὴν (and apostleship). Paul is not an apostle by choice, accident, nor intrusion, but by providence as he has already stated in κλητὸς ἀπόστολος (called apostle, 1:1). His apostleship, even as grace, is "received" from the Lord. Paul names them in their natural order—grace and apostleship. His apostleship is a special grace, and denotes the purpose of his salvation. The chief evidence and highest expression of grace in Paul was his apostleship. This is true not only of an apostle, but of every Christian. Winning the lost is the chief evidence of one's salvation. Evangelism is the highest expression of the saving grace in any individual's soul. That is, grace expresses itself, and missions is its highest expression.

καὶ (and), in connecting χάριν (grace) with ἀποστολὴν (apostleship), forever relates grace with apostleship, blessing with responsibility, ability with obligation, and personal redemption with world missions. God's mercy in salvation becomes a moral obligation to win the lost. The blessing carries a corresponding responsibility. If you have been blessed, you are under obligation to be a blessing. To be a Christian is to be an evangel. Our experience of grace makes us missionary. We are saved, not merely for ourselves but for others. The gospel was given to us on its way to others.   The gospel was given to Paul on its way to the Gentiles.

εἰς ὑπακοὴν . . . (unto obedience of faith among all the nations). The purpose of Paul's grace and apostleship was unto the salvation of the nations. This is the purpose for which he was saved and called.

ὑπὲρ τοῦ ὀνόματος αὐτοῦ (for His name's sake). The final purpose of Paul's grace and apostleship is that Christ's name may be magnified on earth and glorified in heaven. The immediate purpose, in Paul's grace and apostleship, was world redemption; and the final purpose was that the name of Jesus might be glorified above every name. And the glory of Christ is the ultimate purpose of the salvation of the nations.

1:6

ἐν οἷς ἐστε καὶ ὑμεῖς κλητοὶ I. X. (among whom also are ye called ones of Jesus Christ). κλητοὶ is an adjective and should not be translated as if it were a verb. Not "called to be of Jesus Christ," nor "called by Jesus Christ," but "called ones" are His. The genitive of "Jesus Christ" denotes possession. The saved of God are called ones and they belong to Jesus Christ. They are saints because they have been divinely called. They are "called" Christians. (cf. κλητὸς in 1:1).

1:7

In the preceding verses, Paul made due proof of his calling and apostleship for the purpose of introducing himself to his readers. πᾶσιν τοῖς οὖσιν ἐν 'Ρώμῃ (all those that are in Rome) denotes the people to whom he addresses the Epistle. There were both Jews and Gentiles in this church, and they both alike are addressed by Paul as the beloved of God. The implication here is that Paul regards the gospel for all nations, and that the called are beloved of God, whether Jew or Gentile. The merging of the two races into one church gives the anxious apostle a foretaste and a promise of the ultimate realization of the

divine purpose for which he received grace and apostleship: "Unto the obedience of faith in all the nations"
(1:5). Paul sees in this small beginning the guarantee
of world redemption.

πᾶσιν (all) with the article would have denoted the
whole as a unit. The absence of the article denotes the
whole in its variety and multiplicity. The presence of the
article would have denoted the Epistle as addressed to the
church as a body, that is, to the whole congregation of believers as one unit. But Paul omits the article in order
that he might address the whole church, not as a unit, but
in its multiplicity of individual believers. Thus, Paul addresses his Epistle, not to a congregation, but to each individual person in the congregation. The absence of the
article makes the letter specific instead of general, personal instead of relative, individual instead of collective,
personal instead of to the mass. This idea personalizes
his relationship to the Christians at Rome, whom he has
never seen, and enhances the effect upon his readers.
This makes the Epistle as personal as if each believer had
been called by name. (See πάντων [all] in 1:8).

ἀγαπητοῖς θεοῦ (beloved ones of God). The called ones
of Jesus Christ are the loved ones of God. The genitive
θεοῦ (of God) denotes the quality of love as divine. The
genitive also denotes possession—emphasizing the loved
ones as God's possession.

κλητοῖς ἁγίοις (called saints). As Paul was a "called
apostle," so are Christians also "called ones." "Called" is
an adjective without the article, and should not be translated as if it were a verb. The majesty of the saint will be
truly revealed to us, if this expression be interpreted in
the light of the two first paragraphs of the exegesis of
"called apostle" in 1:1. This expression refers the source
and origin of saintship or holiness, back to God in Christ.
The holiness is divine and not of man, imputed and not
personal. "Called saints" or "called holy ones" does not
signify personal holiness, but are so regarded from their
relationship to God as separate from the world and sin,

and further regarded so because of the imputed righteousness of God, by which they are considered justified.
Jesus became sin in order that men through Him might
become the righteousness of God (2 Cor. 5:21). Wherefore, those in Christ are clothed in the righteousness of
God, and are regarded as holy. This expression also re-
nounces salvation by works, and places justification with
Him, Who is holy. "Called saints" denotes imputed righteousness—not that the holy ones are called, but that He
calls man, sinful as he is, to a life of holiness. Furthermore, this expression reveals God as having the initiative
and sovereignty in the salvation of the lost. Man does not
come of himself, pleading his own righteousness by works
of the law; but man is called of God and made holy by
the grace of God's righteousness, divinely imputed. Paul
everywhere attributes salvation, with all its elements, to
God, and nowhere is redemptive credit given to man.
Salvation is of the Lord.

χάρις καὶ εἰρήνη (grace and peace) is an expression used
by Christians in greeting one another. Earlier "peace"
alone was used as the salutation. Christianity added
"grace" to the expression as people received the grace of
God. χάρις (grace) includes all that redemption means,
while εἰρήνη (peace) is the resultant issue of grace. (See
χάριν (grace) in 1:5). Grace denotes the life we have in
Christ, while peace is an inclusive term, summing up the
blessings of this new life in Christ. "Peace" is the truer
term than "prosperity." It denotes peace with God, with
self, and with others. This is the fruit of grace. Grace
and peace are named in their true order. There must be
righteousness before there can be peace. Melchizedek,
king of righteousness, had his throne in Salem, peace.
The name indicates the character of the king, and the
place of his reign denotes the character of his government.

ἀπὸ θεοῦ I. X. (From God our Father and Lord Jesus
Christ). This is the source of grace and peace. Each
word is significant. "God" denotes ability to give, while
"Father" signifies the disposition to give. The character

of God perfects our grace, while the fatherly nature of God insures our peace. The mediator of grace and peace is the Anointed One—Christ, even Jesus, Who made atonement for sin, and is now the Lord of all and head of the new race. He rules for a redemptive purpose, and is able to give every good gift to His own. In Him alone is there grace and peace, and in Him is enough for all.

"God our Father and Lord Jesus Christ" is an important statement in the doctrine of the Person of Christ; but it is not the first doctrinal statement of His Deity in this Epistle, as some seem to imply. Rather it is the summing up of the statements regarding the Deity of Jesus Christ, which are taught in each preceding verse. Paul has already spoken of "His Son," as the Person of the "Gospel of God" (1:1f). Then he said Jesus was the descendant of David, according to the flesh; and that the resurrection proved Him to be the Son of God, according to the Spirit (1:3f). In verse 4f he calls Jesus, Lord, and recognizes Him as the One from Whom he received grace and apostleship. Paul spoke of the "obedience of faith in all nations," in anticipation of the certain universal reign of the Lord Jesus Christ, Whose righteousness shall fill the earth and Whose reign shall be from everlasting to everlasting. In verse 6, Paul says we belong to Jesus Christ, due to our calling. In verse 7, he says that we are called to holiness, that is, Jesus calls and also supplies the needed righteousness. We belong to Him; and we are justified in His righteousness. In the close of this seventh verse, Jesus Christ our Lord is identified with God our Father. Paul has already referred to Jesus as God's Son and our Lord. But here he identifies the Lordship of Jesus Christ with the Fatherhood of God. Wherefore grace is plenteous for the beloved children as they rest under the banner of the Lord of lords.

2. *Thanksgiving and Desire.* 1:8-15

1:8

The Apostle wants his readers to feel his heart beats, as he has felt theirs. This verse establishes a fellowship and Christian unity, even though they have never met. In verse 1, Paul established his apostolic relationship with the Romans, and now he effects the relationship of love.

Paul expresses his thanksgiving towards God for the renown of their faith. His thanksgiving confirms their faith as being a gift from God. He thanks Him Who is the giver of every good gift, and Who alone can give faith (Eph. 2:8f).

περὶ πάντων ὑμῶν (with reference to all of you). The absence of the article calls attention to the multiplicity comprising the whole (cf. πᾶσιν 1:7). That is, Paul is grateful to God through Christ for each individual one in the Roman church. The absence of the article further denotes essence, merit, and character of each individual Christian. The absence of this article, contrasted from the presence of the article with "faith," denotes the multiplicity of individuals comprising the whole to be a unit in the expression of their faith.

ἡ πίστις ὑμῶν (the faith of you). The article with "faith" denotes the unity of their faith. The position of faith before ὑμῶν (of you) places the emphasis upon faith rather than upon whose faith. Paul does not mean to say that the Roman Christians have been renowned to the ends of the earth on account of their faith. It is not the Romans that are renowned. Faith is the thing renowned, and the Romans are mentioned only in that it is their faith that is renowned. He is saying that faith has caught the attention and interest of the whole world, and its being the faith of the Romans is only secondary. The faith of an obscure person can never remain obscure. Much more, Rome being the seat of the world, the whole world was watching her faith.

Paul, informing the Romans that their faith is renowned throughout the whole known world, assures their acceptance of him. For they could not reject the Apostle of God without doing injury to the good will and faithful expectations of all the faithful in the whole world. The Romans must accept Paul wholeheartedly in order to maintain their renown in the eyes of the Christian world. Their self-respect urges their obedience to the teachings that follow in this Epistle. Thus, Paul makes certain that he will be heard and that his doctrine will be believed.

1:9

μάρτυς γάρ μού ἐστιν ὁ θεός (For God is my witness). Paul is absent from his readers, and cannot directly manifest his affection for them. But the love he would lavish upon them must have a channel for its expression. His love finds its outlet in prayer to God for them in addition to his thanksgiving (1:8). Thus, he puts himself upon an oath in order to heighten the intensity of his affection and prayers, and calls upon God, Who alone knows the fullness of his prayer life and the inner secrets of his heart, to be his witness to them in his absence.

ᾧ λατρεύω ἐν τῷ πνεύματί μου (Whom I serve in my spirit). Paul's spirit is the agent of service, and the gospel is the realm or field. He has no other organ of service, nor any other sphere. His serving God in his spirit gives him the authority of Him Who is Spirit, and assures the sincerity of his prayers, and guarantees the validity of his doctrine which is to follow in this Epistle.

λατρεύω (serve) is not the work of a slave, but the service of a priest. In this expression, Paul rises to the height of true priesthood. He is the priest of his own soul—ministering not in a temple, but in his spirit. "God is a Spirit; and they that worship Him must worship Him in spirit and in truth" (John 4:24). Paul's spiritual service does not carry him to the altar to make atonement for others, but "the gospel of His Son" makes every believer a priest—ministering in the spirit through the sacrifice of the Lamb of God, Whose blood was shed for the ransom of many. This expression condemns the external forms and ceremonies in religion, and exalts spiritual service which comes from spiritual life—that life which is evidenced by the testimony of His Spirit with our spirit, that we are the children of God (8:16).

1:10

εἰ πως (if perhaps, if by any means) gives a pessimistic tone to the possibility of his going to Rome even in the future.

ἤδη ποτὲ (before long, at length, if perhaps yet on some distant occasion) indicates that Paul still hopes to make his long delayed journey, even though as yet he sees no possibility.

1:11

ἐπὶ with πόθος does not denote intensity but direction of the longing—to youward.

1:13

The "longing" (1:11) was the genesis of the "purpose" (1:13). Desire led to definite plans for a journey. Love sought a way. Love pursued its object.

1:14

ὀφειλέτης εἰμί (I am debtor). Paul's sense of debtorship does not grow out of any good coming to him from the Gentiles, but from a sense of debt to the Redeemer. His debt to Christ can only be discharged to fallen humanity. Paul has been entrusted with a message that will gloriously meet the need of lost humanity. Because he has it, he is responsible for those in need of it. Need is the genesis of responsibility. Ability is the measure of responsibility. Christian possibilities are Christian responsibilities. Responsibility is not a matter of choice but of equipment. A blessing carries a corresponding responsibility (cf. Gen. 12:2). Responsibility arises out of relationship. The relationship of the lost to us is that of need; our relationship to the lost is that of debtorship; our relationship to God is that of a steward, who must one day give an account of his stewardship.

Ἕλλησίν τε καὶ βαρβάροις (both to Greeks and to Barbarians). Paul used this term to express the universality of his debtorship. The term included all Gentiles in their diversity of languages. The Greeks used the term to include all people. The Jews used it to include all Gentiles, while they employed "Jew and Greek" (1:16) to include all mankind. Paul used this expression to classify all nations; but the emphasis of the classification was upon Greek culture rather than upon nationality. Thus, Paul included his readers among the Greeks and the wise.

The βαρβάροις (Barbarians) are those whose speech is rude, rough, and harsh, as if repeating the syllable: bar, bar; hence one who speaks a foreign or strange language, that is, a language that is not understood. The term was used more specifically to denote all non-Greeks. Though both the Greeks and Jews applied the term each to the other.

These very words, from the pen of Paul, are prophetic of the universality of his ministry. For Paul is a Jew writing in Greek to the Latins. Thus, in the writing of these words, Paul has a foretaste of the glories of his ministry, and in it sees a ray of hope whereby his debtorship is to be discharged to the world in its universality.

The three all-inclusive languages of the world, which proclaimed the Kingship of Jesus by the inscription on the cross, are now embodied in a Hebrew apostle, writing Greek to a Roman world, declaring the servant of the King to be in debt to the same three inclusive races of the world, that is, mankind in its universality. The inscription, in the three languages, denotes every language as crucifying Jesus, and now Paul says that people of every language may have the righteousness provided by that sacrificial death on the cross.

σοφοῖς τε καὶ ἀνοήτοις (both to the wise and to the foolish). As Paul's ministry to the Gentiles is unrestricted as to races, nationality, and language, his ministry is furthermore dedicated to these people without respect to degree of culture or intellect. All need it—the wise and the unwise, the learned and the unlearned, the cultured and the crude, the intelligent and the ignorant, the civilized and the uncivilized; and the gospel is for all alike irrespective as to degree of mental ability or attainment. The wisdom of the cultured will not save, nor can it find the way to God, for as they profess themselves to be wise, they become fools (1:22) ; and the ignorant are inexcusable. God "will destroy the wisdom of the wise, and bring to naught the understanding of the prudent" (I Cor. 1:19; cf. Job 5:12-15) ; and the ignorant shall glory in the "excellency of the knowledge of Christ Jesus" (Phil. 3:8), and shall be satisfied with "the peace of God, which passeth all understanding" (Phil. 4:7). The wise must turn from their wisdom and know only Jesus, and the ignorant have the supreme knowledge in Him—for to know Him is life eternal (cf. John 17:3).

1:15

οὕτω τὸ κατ' ἐμὲ (So, as much as in me is). Paul feels the enormity of his debt to the lost world—an infinite debt, one that could never be fully discharged. He seems to intimate that the task is more than human. Paul pledges that the limit of his world conquest shall be no less than the full measure of himself. As far as it is humanly possible, his accomplishment will measure up to his goal. He will pay on the debt until all his rescources are exhausted in death. He is ready to apply all he is on his debt to the Gentiles. The life of Paul, as we get it through his Epistles, gives evidence that his labors measured up to his matchless ability.

πρόθυμον (ready—πρό and θυμός). This adjective describes Paul's eagerness to preach the gospel to those in Rome. θυμός means to be in a heat, as from running; to have anger or fury. It reveals violent breathing, as a man in a rage, as anger repeatedly boiling up and subsiding again. The angry, distressed, or eager man breathes violently and pants heavily and rapidly. The violent raging, the short, rapid, and heavy breathing of a parent, when the child is endangered, gives an idea of Paul's exasperation to preach the gospel in Rome. The heat of the runner, the fury of an angry man, the bursting of flames, the uncontrolled breathing of a distressed parent, all express Paul's overwhelming passion to preach the unsearchable riches of His grace. Thus, did Paul want to preach. Passionate preaching is the success of the ministry.

εὐγγελίσασθαι (to preach). The infinitive is in the aorist tense. The aorist is the decisive tense, the tense of finality and absoluteness. Paul had a gospel of absoluteness, of certainties, and a message of finality. Paul did not preach in generalities and platitudes. He had a definite gospel that was absolute in its realm and final in its revelation. He did not hesitate to say that he had the last word as to salvation. Paul preached the authoritative gospel with authority. The infinitive shows purpose and determination.

3. The Thesis of the Epistle. 1:16-17

1:16

οὐ ἐπαισχύνομαι (I am not ashamed). This is a negative proof of his being ready (1:15). Paul is conscious of his sufferings, in both body and spirit, from the hands of those who are ashamed of the gospel of the cross. The attitude of sinful men cannot make the cross offensive to Paul. He knows that the cross is "unto Jews a stumbling block, and unto Greeks foolishness," and furthermore, he knows that "unto them which are called, both Jews and Greeks, Christ the power of God, and the wisdom of God" (I Cor. 1:23f).

τὸ εὐαγγέλιον (the gospel) is the gospel message itself, and not the act of carrying or preaching the gospel.

δύναμις θεοῦ (divine power, power of God). ἐνέργεια

(work, energy) denotes the activity of power, but δύναμις (power) refers to the source of power. This power is inherent in the nature of God. And the nature of God is the only power that can give life to the lost. The Law was never called power, but Grace "is the power of God unto salvation to every one that believeth."

παντὶ τῷ πιστεύοντι (to every one who believes). The absence of the article from παντὶ (all; cf.1:7f) denotes the individuality among the whole. This power of God is manifested to each separately and individually, not to a group, tribe, or nation; and that only as the individual believes. Personal responsibility to the gospel through faith is emphasized. Second, the absence of the article denotes the universality of the gospel through faith— every one, each one, any one (3:22). In the third place, it alludes to the equality of all sinners—each separately, but any one, all alike—in faith. Thus, the absence of the article shows individuality, universality, and equality.

'Ιουδαίῳ τε πρῶτον . . . (to the Jew first and also to the Greek). "Greeks" includes all Gentiles, and "Jew and Greek" includes all mankind. καὶ (and), a co-ordinate conjunction, denotes the equality of the Gentiles with the Jews in gospel privileges and grace.

The gospel was divinely appointed to be first preached to the Jews, and then to be given equally to the Gentiles. The Messiah was promised as the seed of Abraham and to be the Son of David, and to sit upon His father's throne. From the very nature of the promise of the Messiah, it was only natural that the gospel should be first preached to the Jews. Not that the Jews had any pre-eminence in privilege or grace; but of inevitable necessity, the Messianic message must first be proclaimed by and to those who first have the Messiah. And yet the emphasis is not upon the point of time, but rather upon the responsibility of leadership in the proclamation of the gospel. Paul is glad to refer the priority of responsibility to the Jews in the form of a compliment, in order that this might be a shield in warding off later attacks from the Jews upon certain doctrines in the Epistle.

1:17

δικαιοσύνη θεοῦ. "A divine righteousness" is a true translation by use of the absence of the Greek article. This does not mean a righteousness from God, though it is from Him, but the righteousness is God's essence, His character. God gives Himself to make sinners righteous. Man is acceptable, being clothed in God's righteousness.

Man has no righteousness. Yet he can not be saved without it. And man can not produce a righteousness. This is proven by the corrupt Gentiles, and by the Jews with the Law. For man is dead—dead in sin and trespasses (Eph. 2:1). He is the victim of sin, an enemy to God, and a servant of Satan. Only God has righteousness, and He offers His own righteousness to unrighteous men, as the only means whereby they can be saved. This scripture is clear that man has no righteousness of his own, that there is only one source of righteousness, that that righteousness is the only condition of salvation, and that faith is the only means by which God can give His righteousness to us. Therefore, man is not saved by works of his own righteousness, for he has none; but by the divine work of grace in God's righteousness. Salvation is of the Lord and not of man. God does the saving, and He does it with His righteousness.

One might ask how much of God's righteousness would be proportioned to each believer, seeing there are multiplied millions of redeemed people through the ages. This question can be asked only by one who does not understand God's infinity. The emphasis of omnipresence is not that God is present everywhere, but that all of God is present here, now, all the time. The idea is not that God is scattered throughout the universe, but that all of God is present at every point in the universe. You have all the presence of God all the time; and God is all to you that He could be, were you the only human being in the universe. Wherefore, the multiplied millions is no more strain upon God's righteousness than if you were the only one drawing on the infinite and inexhaustible supply. Likewise, all His righteousness is the supply to each believer, as if he were the only recipient of God's righteousness. If you were the only one ever saved, God's grace and righteousness could not be richer nor fuller to you than now. The righteousness of God is not diminished by its liberality. And there is no less of His righteousness for you, however abundantly He shall multiply His grace to others.

ἐκ πίστεως εἰς πίστιν (out of faith unto faith) denotes a growing faith. But more specifically does it denote the means whereby a man obtains the righteousness of God for himself. This is a faith-righteousness set over in opposition to a work-righteousness. It is not a work-righteousness to be had by deeds nor by obedience to law, but it is a faith-righteousness to be had by the grace of God through faith (Eph. 2:8f). Faith is the only way God's righteousness can be had, and faith is the only way salvation can be to "whosoever will."

Paul quotes Habakkuk 2:4 to show that the faith-righteousness is not a new doctrine. Faith has always been connected with righteousness, and this has always been God's way.

DOCTRINAL

1:18-8:39

II. THE DOCTRINE OF SIN. 1:18-3:20.

III. THE DOCTRINE OF JUSTIFICATION. 3:21-5:21.

IV. THE DOCTRINE OF SANCTIFICATION. 6:1-8:39.

II

THE DOCTRINE OF SIN

1:18—3:20

I. THE GENTILES ARE CONDEMNED WITHOUT THE LAW

1:18-32

1. The Truth of God held down. 1:18-23.
    (1) The Gentiles were corrupt in practice. 1:18-20.
    (2) They became corrupt in thinking. 1:21f.
    (3) They became corrupt in their worship. 1:23.

2. The Wrath of God revealed by His giving up the Gentiles. 1:24-32.
    (1) For wrong loving. 1:24f.
    (2) For wrong living. 1:26f.
    (3) For wrong thinking. 1:28-32.

1. *The Truth of God held down.* 1:18-23

1:18

Verse 16 declares the gospel to be "the power of God unto salvation." Verse 17 explains that power to be God's righteousness for unrighteous men appropriated through faith. Paul's purpose in the remainder of this chapter and through 3:20 is to prove that man has no righteousness and is incapable of producing a righteousness, except as it is imputed to him from God. The remainder of this chapter deals with the corrupt and condemned Gentiles, while the second chapter brings like guilt and condemnation upon the Jews. 3:1-20 shows universal corruption and condemnation upon man.

In addition to having no righteousness, man is condemned, justly condemned, condemned of God; and the wrath, the holy wrath of God, is upon him. Man died in sin; so life must be regenerated in righteousness imputed

through faith; then all, who have no righteousness except
their own, are without righteousness, without faith, without life, and are dead—died under guilt and condemnation. There is the revelation of the righteousness of
God (1:17), and there is the counterpart of it—the revelation of the wrath of God. Now in order to induce man
to come to God's righteousness, and to justify writing on
the theme, Paul proves that man is personally guilty,
altogether unrighteous, justly and divinely condemned,
and that the only life, only salvation, and only righteousness for him is the righteousness of God through faith.
The need of righteousness ought to bring man to the
source of all righteousness. Man's guilt ought to draw
him to the Liberator. His condemnation ought to lead
him to the Great Deliverer. The wrath of God ought to
drive him to the love of God. His groping in the dark
ought to teach man the need and value of the Light of the
World. His lack of righteousness ought to reveal to him
the absolute necessity of the righteousness of God. Sin
ought to drive a man to seek salvation. The revelation of
wrath ought to scourge sinners to the revelation of righteousness.

'Αποκαλύπτεται γὰρ ὀργὴ θεοῦ (For there is a wrath of God
revealed). The absence of the article from θεοῦ (God)
denotes the nature of the wrath. The wrath of God does
not have in it the ugly, sinful, hateful nature that is manifested in the human anger. The anger of God is only the
reaction of the love of a Holy God in the presence of sin.
θεοῦ (God), without the article, signfies "a divine wrath."
The absence of the article denotes "wrath"to be the nature
of God; that is, it is His nature to react against sin. This
characterizes the wrath as divine, that is, this attitude
towards sinful man is the inevitable reaction of God's
holy nature. Only wrath could be exhibited towards sin
and God remain consistent with Himself. The term
"wrath" designates the reaction that is inherent in the
essential nature of Deity with reference to sin. Wrath
against unrighteousness is as natural to the nature of

God as His approval of holiness. Wrath is as natural to the nature of God as is His love. He could not be holy without being jealous for His holiness. He could not be holy without reacting against sin. He could not be inconsistent with His holiness and remain holy. This wrath is in perfect harmony with His Deity. It is His righteousness acting consistently with itself in the presence of sin. Since this wrath is in God's essential deity and grows out of His holiness, it is just to man, and man is guilty, and therefore under condemnation. Where there is faith in God, there is the revelation of the righteousness of God (1:17); where there is no faith, but unbelief with its issues, there is the revelation of the wrath of God. The one statement is the counterpart of the other statement. The revelation of the one would necessitate the revelation of the other.

ἀπ' οὐρανοῦ (from heaven). Heaven is the dwelling place and throne of God, but that interpretation would only weaken the import of this revelation. θεοῦ (God; rather, divine—being without the article) is the nature of the wrath; and οὐρανοῦ (heaven) is the source of the wrath. Therefore, the reaction against sin is not from God alone; "heaven" without the article shows that all heaven reacts with God against all sin. All heaven is in unity in God's wrath against "all ungodliness and immorality of men." Therefore, God acts to the full power of all heaven in revealing His wrath upon ungodly men. All heaven is behind the revealed wrath.

ἀσέβειαν καὶ ἀδικίαν (ungodliness and immorality). ἀσέβειαν (ungodliness, or irreverence) denotes the lack of reverence toward God, impiety, ungodliness, both in thought and deed. This word as used in the Septuagint Greek translation corresponds to the Hebrew, פָּשַׁע, to be rebellious, out of harmony morally and spiritually with God, turbulent, etc. ἀδικίαν denotes injustice, unrighteousness, immorality in heart and life. The two words denote irreverence towards God and immorality with reference to man. The first word has no fear for the Lord; the second, no standard for man. The first denies God's character; the second destroys man's character. The first word attacks the person of God; the second attacks His government. The first term would destroy the existence of God; the second would destroy the existence of man. The first word condemns God; the second seeks to justify man for his irreverence.

κατεχόντων (holding down). The participle denotes a continuous action. They were consistent in their sins. They persevered in their immorality. The article with "truth" denotes a particular truth; one that was clear, comprehensible, unified, that is, consistent, well understood, not indefinite, not hazy. The article gives individuality to this truth as being pre-eminent among all facts. The pre-eminence of this truth is so stated as to denote its being the one truth, the whole of truth, the only truth. We could almost say the article personalizes the truth. It does show that wicked men fought the truth of God with all the hate and malice that could be mustered against a person. They fought the living truth as a living enemy.

Corrupt men used the most deadly weapon against truth. Truth can survive swords, it can battle down ignorance, and overcome prejudice; but truth is defeated in immorality. They held down the truth of God by their immorality. Truth can only live in the minds of people as it lives in the lives of people; and when it dies in the lives of people, it dies to their knowledge. That is why character and thought have such close relationship. Thus, an immoral life corrupts mind. The mind of an immoral man is not safe. Sound judgment must be accompanied by a pure heart. There is an affinity between righteousness and knowledge, between purity of life and clearness of thought.

Those who "hold down the truth" are just as much liars as those who pervert the truth. To pervert, cover, change, conceal, or withhold the truth is to lie. To hold down the greatest truth is the biggest lie. God is the biggest truth, and to live as if there were no God is to live the biggest lie.

1:19

διότι τὸ γνωστὸν τοῦ θεοῦ φανερόν ἐστιν ἐν αὐτοῖς (Because the revealed knowledge of the God is within them). The strongest inferential particle is used here. φαερόν (manifest or reveal) is an adjective and not a verb, and should be so translated. Therefore, the clause does not mean "that which is knowable," nor "what may be known," but "revealed knowledge."

The presence of the article with θεοῦ (God) denotes personality. They had revealed knowledge of the Personal God. They knew Him as a Person. The following verses say they knew Him as Creator, as Omnipotence, and as Deity. But the article here says they knew Him in Person—as a Personal God. Therefore, they are guilty without excuse, and the wrath of God is righteous and just.

"Is within them." The force of this clause is not that the knowledge of God was revealed to them, but that the knowledge of God is within them by virtue of inherent existence, and as an abiding principle of their nature. "Is" denotes the divinely revealed knowledge to inherently exist as an abiding principle within the consciousness of man. "Within" expresses the realm of God's inefface- able revelation—within, in their hearts, upon the consciousness, within the Ego.

The truth of God was revealed, not among them, but within them—upon their consciousness, in their hearts (2:15). The truth of God is vividly manifested, revealed, exhibited openly, shown plainly, laid clearly or openly within them. This revelation came from the personality of God to the inner consciousness of man. What more could God do? How more guilty could man be? Man revolted against God from the very seat of his being.

The remainder of this verse says "for God manifested it unto them." If God wrote Himself into human consciousness and upon the tablets of their hearts, then the revelation was perfect. The revelation registered in their consciousness, "for God manifested it unto them." Inspiration has just said: "that which is known of God is manifest within them." The present tense alludes to the permanency of that knowledge in human consciousness. Now, the Spirit says through Paul, "For God manifested it unto them" (ἐφανέρωσεν). The aorist tense shows the act as wrought once for all. When God stamped the knowledge of Himself upon human consciousness, He did it once for all time; that is, no human being has ever been without that knowledge. It is an inherent element in the nature of man. This is the explanation for the universal thirst for God. That is why man must worship, and why the heathen do worship—something. Immorality will defeat the truth of God, but it can never obliterate it from human nature.

1:20

γὰρ ἀόρατα αὐτοῦ (For the invisible things of him).   In the former verse, God gave the revelation of Himself direct and subjectively.   In this verse, the revelation is given objectively through creation.   The evidences of the first revelation may be reached through the second—making man doubly inexcusable.   Man ought to have found the Fatherhood of God in the sparrow's nest.   He could have seen the providence of God in His feeding the birds, and in His painting of the flowers. And from these things, man could have known God's loving care for the priceless souls of men.

The invisible attributes that constitute God's nature are enumerated in this verse under three heads: (1) Eternal One, (2) Omnipotence, and (3) Divinity.   The creation teaches the eternity of the Creator, by the simple law of cause and effect, and God could not create Himself. God's creative power could not be seen, but His visible creation is evidence of the creative power, for the world could not exist by chance, that is, without a source.   His government of the world is proof of His love, mercy, goodness, etc., summed up in the one word "Divinity."

εἰς τὸ (to the end that).   The everlasting power and divinity are revealed in order that guilty man may be found defenseless and without testimony against the justice of God before the eternal tribunal of heaven.

1:21

διότι γνόντες τὸν θεὸν (because that, knowing God). Again the strongest inferential particle is used. The aorist participle denotes the permanency of the knowledge of the Personal God. No depth of moral degradation at any time in the future can wholly blot out the knowledge of God. The heathen are responsible now.

οὖν ἐδόξασαν ἢ ηὐχαρίστησαν (neither glorified nor gave thanks). Both verbs are aorist active indicative. The indicative mood states the appalling fact. The active voice reveals their progressiveness in this double sin. The aorist expresses the resolute and final decisiveness with which they refused the due adoration to God. Their refusal was decisive: It had determination in it. They refused with violence. "The praising and thanksgiving exhaust the notion of the adoration, which they should have offered to God." (Meyer). "Glory" is the manifestation of that which is valuable. The glitter is not the gold; it is the glory of the value. We translate δόξα, glory; but the chief idea must ever be upon the value that produces the glory. The root idea is value. They did not value God. They did not glorify God, that is, they did not give Him an evaluation in their lives. Then the Apostle gets a little more personal and says they did not give God any evaluation in their hearts, in that they did not offer thanks to Him.

ἀλλὰ (but) is the strongest conjunction. It denotes the strictest contrast between what they ought to have done and what they did.

ἐματαιώθησαν. Not "they became vain," but "they were made vain." The passive voice is an implication of the personality of Satan. Forsaking the truth of God, they turned to the vanity of their own reasoning. The vanity was in their mind. The next expression shows the disorder to

have entered the heart—the seat of their moral nature
and the center of their personality.

ἐσκοτίσθη ἡ ἀσύνετος αὐτῶν καρδία (their senseless heart was
darkened). They could not see things in their proper relation, nor could they rightly evaluate them. They were
unable to make moral and spiritual discriminations. When
they refused to follow the light, they wandered in darkness. When they revolted against truth, their minds had
an affinity for falsehood and error. Their refusal of
truth incapacitated them mentally. Man can not arrive at
moral truths except in the light of the Great Truth. He
who does not know the truth does not know what is right;
and he who does not want the truth does not want to
know what is right. Truth and right go hand in hand.
The mind that does not live in relation to the truth of
God is so warped and withered by sin (Ps.14:1), that it is
incapable of discriminating between truth and error, or
good and evil. Through the dullness of their stupidity,
self-imposed through their immorality, they lost the revelation of God through nature, but they did not lose the
revelation of God from their Ego, for there are none so
steeped in sin and heathenism as to have no conception
of some deity and worship of the same. God ineffaceably
stamped it upon them (1:19).

καρδία (heart). The heart denotes the center of all
moral and spiritual understanding, emotion, will, and activity. καρδία, Hebrew, לֵב (heart), lays emphasis upon
the center of the personality, as the physical heart is the
center of the body. This is an all-inclusive term for the
human faculties; it is the seat of reason, thought (10:6,
8), will (1 Cor. 4:5; 7:37; Romans 14:18), and emotion
(9:2; 10:1). The heart is the center of man's moral and
spiritual nature. It gives moral character to the whole
personality, whether it is the home of sin (1:24), or of
the Spirit (5:5).

1:22

φάσκοντες (professing). This profession grew out of (1)
a false conceit of wisdom (cf. 1 Cor. 1:17ff), (2) vain

thinking and reasoning, and (3) out of a stupid heart darkened in depravity—a heart and mind hardened, twisted, dwarfed, warped, and withered in immorality.

ἐμωράνθησαν (were made fools) is aorist tense and passive voice. The aorist expresses the resolute and final decisiveness with which they were made fools. The passive voice forbids rendering this word, "they became fools"; but correctly translates it, "they were made fools." The passive voice is an implication of the personality of Satan. "Professing themselves to be wise, they were made fools"; that is, the more of their wisdom they exercised the bigger fools they were made. Following what they thought to be wise led them deeper into folly. Giving heed to their wisdom would make fools of any people.

1:23

ἤλλαξαν (changed, altered, modified, imitated). In this word is the idea of "imitation." This would only heighten their guilt. They did not turn to idolatry ignorantly, nor because they had no conception of God, nor because they knew nothing else to worship. They willfully became idolators, and imitated their deities and worship after the true God. They "imitated" His glory for images of man, birds, beasts, and reptiles. The idea of imitation can be seen in the English word "changed." If they had not known the true God, idolatry would have been an invention instead of a revision. Idolatry is the product of vain minds and darkened hearts, as they imitated the true God in their false deities. Idolatry did not come through ignorance; it is the imitation of what they knew of God. Idolatry is not the religion of an ignorant people; it is the religion of a wicked people. They are responsible, and are therefore guilty without excuse.

The wickedness of idolatry is more than the sins of idolatry; it is a false representation of the true God. They imitated the glory or value of God to make a counterfeit religion. A false representation of God produces false character. The perishing images deny the incorruptible-ness of God. The presence of the idol falsely represents the omnipotence of God. And mortal man can give no conception of the eternity of God. The cold marble misrepresents the loving mercy of the Father. The helpless wood does not teach of His power to help us. The silent deities do not encourage prayer nor call for fellowship. "They that make them (idols) are like unto them" (Ps. 115:8). Man is like his God (or idols). Man is no better than his idea of God (or idols). Man cannot rise above his idol; if he should, he would discredit it and cast it away. And man's conception of God (or his idols) determines his relation to his fellow man.

As the heathen seek to imitate the glory of God for their images, they more nearly project human personality into immensity with all their sins and faults. Therefore, the idol is a magnified sinner, and idolatry becomes the totality of their sins. Whereby, any of their vileness can be glorified by inculcating it into their religion. For where did the heathen get the sex idea with reference to their deities, except from their own practices? And as they have applied the sex idea to their deities, they have exalted adultery and prostitution into their religion as acts of worship.

The very fact that the heathen make images, and worship idols, and offer sacrifices upon altars show that man needs a sacrifice, that there is a God who ought to be worshiped, that they are depraved and can not save themselves, and that salvation belongs to another—unto God.

The idols had soon and long ceased to be images of man, but were in the likeness of an image of man—not in the likeness of man, but in the likeness of an image—of man. The idols were not made in the image of man, but after the likeness of an image. There are no idols that look like a man. They were not formed after a man, but after images—until they have lost all that is even human, and look so hideous that they rather suggest demons. So in this verse we see how far idolatry has fallen short of even a fair representation of man, to say nothing of the likeness and image of God. The "likeness of an image" is the antipode of "the glory of the incorruptible Personal God." The degradation of the idolatrous worship is shown in the downward grade from the likeness of an image of man, fowls, beasts, to reptiles.

2. *The Wrath of God revealed by His giving up the Gentiles.* 1:24-32

1:24

παρέδωκεν (gave up). This word is used three times—here, and in verses 26 and 28. Idolatry leads to all forms of moral degradation. God gave them up (1) for wrong loving (1:24f), (2) for wrong living (1:26f), and (3) for wrong thinking (1:28-32).

ἐν ταῖς ἐπιθυμίαις (in their lusts, or in their vile passions). This denotes their desire, longing, lust, love, and affection. Their lust came from the seat of affection. They loved the forbidden. They were unclean, immoral, and vile in what they loved. God gave them up unto their vile affections. The plural denotes the many avenues they practiced in the expression of their affection. The vileness of lust was what they loved most. But the emphasis is upon the fact that their love and affection degenerated in its expression to the vileness of unrestrained passion running rampant.

ἐν (in) denotes "the vile passions" to be the realm in which they lived, and God gave them up to remain in their vile affections. "Their hearts"reveals the source and seat of the lust. The heart is more than the center of their nature; it is the whole of their personality. "Their bodies" designates the nature of their unchastity. Their impurity culminated in the physical.

ἐν αὐτοῖς (among themselves) charges more than one as participating in the disgraceful expression of a degenerate affection in sensuality.

God punished their sins by giving them over to more sins. They were punished by having the desire of their hearts. One of the Old Testament words for "punishment" is a word for "sin." When Cain said, "My punishment is greater than I can bear" (Gen. 4:13), he literally said, "My 'sin' is greater than I can bear." Isaiah 1:31 teaches that the sin of the sinner will be his destruction.

1:25

μετήλλαξαν τὴν ἀλήθειαν τοῦ θεοῦ ἐν τῷ ψεύδει (they exchanged the truth of God for a lie). They imitated (changed) the glory of God for their images (1:23) ; but "exchanged" declares that there is no truth embodied in idolatry and that there is no truth to which it can lead. Foreign missionaries tell us that it is impossible to win the heathen by explaining God in terms of idolatry or by using the knowledge of their gods as a stepping-stone to the knowledge of the living God. The knowledge of their deities is of no advantage in forming a conception of Jehovah. The only time Paul failed was when he preached to the Athenians, basing the knowledge of the true God upon their "unknown god" (Acts 17:23). To Paul, it looked like an opportunity, but he woefully failed. He never repeated the strategy. Idolatry can not imitate the divine reality of God. It is the negation of the truth of God.

ἐσεβάσθησαν καὶ ἐλάτρευσαν (worshipped and served). The first word denotes reverence or worship. For a discussion of this word see "irreverence" in 1:18. The latter word expresses the activity of the first, and denotes the offering of sacrifiices. For a discussion of this word see 1:9.

παρὰ (with, by the side of). Here it denotes the other side, the wrong side as opposed to the right side. It carries the idea that they "passed up" the Creator, in order to worship and serve the creatures. The Creator was the first in order of choice or rejection. God was "passed up," after which idolatry was chosen. In 1:18, the truth of God was "held down," and now we see God is "passed up." When man "holds down" the truth of God, the next step in the growth of sin is to "pass up" God.

ὅς ἐστιν εὐλογητὸς (Who is blessed). The riches of God's grace contrasted from the horrors of the subjects of His wrath drew from Paul a doxology at a most unlikely time.

1:26f

Verses 1:26f describe their wrong living which grew out of their wrong loving in 1:24f. What people do grows directly out of what they love. Idolatry brings unnatural sins out of natural desires. Paul does not call them "men and women," but associates them with beasts by referring to them as "females and males." Paul first mentions the horror of the "females," because modesty is woman's most beautiful adornment (1 Tim. 2:9). He speaks of women with women, and men with men, abusing their sex. The beastly sins are a direct result of their choosing a lie. The horror of idolatry is not its ignorance, but its sin.

1:28

οὐκ ἐδοκίμασαν is translated "refused." The verb means to think, consider, or value. ("Glory" in 1:21, comes from the same root.) They did not think God, so God gave them up to degenerate thinking. God did not inflict them with a reprobate mind, but gave them over to the reprobate mind that they had acquired in casting God out of their thinking. As the Gentiles refused to have God in their knowledge, God refused to have them in His knowledge. They did not value God, and God gave them up to a reprobate mind. They did not value God (1:21), and in turn God did not value them. No one is of value, who does not value God. As they thought God to be worthless, God delivered them up to a worthless mind. As they cast God out of their minds, God gave them up to an outcast mind. They became of no value when they refused to value God. When they refused to evaluate God, He refused to evaluate them. When they considered God to be worthless, God declared them worthless. Wrong loving (1:24f) and wrong living (1:26f) leads to wrong thinking (1:28-32).

And any system of education that casts God out is an outcast type of education. Education that does not value

God is a worthless education. A godless training is a worthless course, and a wicked study—study in wickedness. Instruction away from God is not edification. There is no true philosophy that makes an outcast of theology. There is no valuable scholarship which casts God out of the realm of values. There is no true science separate and apart from omniscience. And there is no wisdom in the instruction, that is antagonistic to the mind of God.

1:29-31

πεπληρωμένους (having been filled). The perfect participle denotes the present possession of past accomplishments. The significance is that the vices had become hard and permanent traits of character. Therefore, the catalogue of sins in these verses are not deeds of impulse, but the sins of long formed character. The enumerated sins in these verses are not strange terms. Thayer's Greek Lexicon is clear on all these words.

1:32

This verse is the summary of verses 1:18-31, and at the same time is a transition into the next division of thought. Being unable to make moral distinctions, they became well pleased with their vices though they knew the law of God to be against all immorality.

συνευδοκοῦσιν means to consider well among one another, together deeming the value to be good, to agree that the value is desirable, and to think well of one another in their sinful practice. "Think" and "value" are both in this verb. The index of character is not so much what a man indulges in as what he considers well in those who do indulge. They considered the things mentioned in verses 1:29ff to be of greater value than God (1:21, 28, 32), and thought more of others for their like thinking.

II. THE JEWS ARE CONDEMNED WITH THE LAW
2:1-29

1. God judges according to truth. 2:1-5.
2. God judges according to works. 2:6-10.
3. God judges without respect of person. 2:11-15.
4. God judges according to Paul's gospel. 2:16.
5. God judges according to light. 2.17-25.
6. God judges according to the heart. 2:26-29.

1. *God judges according to truth.* 2:1-5

2:1

ἀναπολόγητος (without a word, without an answer, without excuse). The Jew felt that a part of his righteousness consisted in condemning others (Luke 18:11; Gal. 2:15). He made moral distinctions. He declared himself a reliable judge on moral behavior. Therefore, as he condemned Gentile wickedness and approved divine wrath, it is thereby evidenced that he knows both what is right, and what is wrong. Thus, he knows that such practice is condemned by the lower court of man and by the higher court of God. The Jew is guilty without defence, being skilled in moral distinctions through practice and through observing God's discriminations made through favor and wrath.

ὦ ἄνθρωπε (O Man). This word carries the generic sense of humanity. It does not denote gender, but is inclusive of all humanity. We use "man" in the same sense to include men, women, and children. The use of the generic in the singular personalizes all the Jews as one man. It further denotes the multiplicity of Jews to have judged as if by one man's voice; that is, their judgment was one. The universality of the Jews was a unity in expressed judgment upon Gentile immorality. Furthermore, this word individualizes the collective whole, in order that all will be as one in the judgment. The multiplicity is unified in one guilt, and thereby only one judgment is necessitated. There is also in this word the implication of all humanity—unifying both Jew and Gentile as one man, in one and the same guilt, and coming to one and the same judgment.

σεαυτὸν κατακρίνεις (thou condemnest thyself). The idea of the individualized whole is still retained. He that reproves stealing, condemns theft in every one—including his own thieving. In condemning Gentile sins, he sentences himself in like condemnation, because he commits like sins. Likewise, in approving God's wrath upon the Gentiles, he is sentencing himself to the same divine judgment for like practices.

τὰ αὐτὰ πράσσεις (practice the same things). Paul does not mean that the Jew is guilty of all the Gentile immorality (1:18-32) ; yet the Jew was grossly guilty of many of the viler sins common among Gentiles. In 2:21-24, many of the common and well known sins among the Jews are enumerated under the heads of theft, adultery, idolatry, lawlessness, and blasphemy. Josephus records much Jewish history that reads like Gentile criminality. Paul does mean to say that the Jew sinned against revelation in conscience, against revelation in nature, against God's will revealed in the Law, against mercy shown among Jews, and against knowledge obtained from observing God's wrath among Gentiles. The sins of the Jews were not identical with Gentile sins; but their sin was the same—both sinned against light. The Gentile is without excuse, and much more is the Jew, since he does the same things—sinning against greater light.

2:2

οἴδαμεν (We know). γινώσκω denotes a knowledge grounded in personal experience, experiential knowledge, that revealed through inner experience. οἶδα is from εἴδω, to see, to perceive with the eye. The emphasis is upon eyesight. It denotes eye-witness in contrast to knowledge imparted from others. And when the perception registers, it becomes knowledge (οἶδα). Thus οἴδαμεν (we know) denotes external evidence. Paul is saying that "We know by observation that the judgment of God is according to truth." Through the mercy of God, the Jews did not know (γινώσκω) experientially. But through the visitations of divine wrath upon Gentile immorality, they knew (οἴδαμεν) from observations, from examples, from personal eye-witness, and from calamities seen with their own eyes. That which came under the observation of their eyes gave conclusive knowledge that "the judgment of God is according to truth." Paul so framed his statement as to admit no denial by any one who has eyes. And he states this knowledge to be already in the possession of every one, and coexistent with their eyes. Paul establishes his statement by making their eyes the proof of their knowledge.

τὸ κρίμα τσῦ θεοῦ (the judgment of God). "The judgment of God according to truth" is contrasted so as to condemn the human judgment which is so inconsistent with their carnal living.

The absence of the article from "wrath" (1:18) revealed the visitation of penalties for sins to be in a general and varied way. The time of the wrath is both present and indefinite—the time of wrath being determined by the occasion and time of the sins; that is, the revelation of divine wrath chronologically accompanied every expression of sin. The article is present with "judgment," and denotes more than a repetition of such wrath as was upon the Gentiles. "The judgment" is a special and final occasion for the pouring out of God's wrath in all its fullness. This judgment is future, full, and final. It is the Great Judgment Day, when the righteous shall be rewarded by "Come, ye blessed of my Father, inherit the kingdom prepared for you from the foundation of the world" (Matt. 25:34), and the wicked shall hear their sentence: "Depart from me, ye cursed, into everlasting fire, prepared for the devil and his angels" (Matt. 25:41).

In 1:18, the article was absent from "God." This characterized the nature of the wrath as being divine. But the article is present with "God" in the verse under consideration. The article introduces the Judge. The Judge is a Person—the Personal God. The judgment of God is to be more personal than the wrath of God (1:18), as is shown by the presence and absence of the article respectively.

As God manifested His wrath against the Gentiles, He let their own sins be a part of their punishment (1:24). But the recoil of sins is not all the judgment. And all of a sinner's condemnation does not come from natural causes, nor from his own convulsive conscience, nor from the torment of devouring sins. But the awful judgment shall be personal. The personal sinner shall be tried personally before the Personal Judge—the Great Jehovah, fearful as a lion, loving as a father, judging according to truth.

κατὰ ἀλήθειαν (according to truth). In 1:25, "truth" referred to the reality of the personal God. In this verse, "truth" has a different meaning. Here it refers to man rather than to God; and more particularly does it refer to the Jews. The Scripture does not say God judges according to His reality, but that He judges according to the reality in man; that is, according to man's real nature. "Truth" often means sincerity of mind and integrity of character (cf. John 8:44). In this instance, "truth" is the actual condition or inner reality of the man judged.

Truth does not denote the standard of judgment, but the method of judging. The standard is Christ; that is, man must by faith live in harmony with the Divine Truth. But with reference to the Christ-standard, God will judge the heart, and not the outward forms of religion (2:16, 28f). He will judge according to inward sincerity and not according to hypocritical profession; according to reality and not according to formality. In the Great Judgment Day, no sentence will be rendered upon the basis of anything outward nor external. Neither will salvation rest upon ceremonies, forms, rites, circumcision, church membership, nor baptism. Formal sanctity can not hide secret sins from His all seeing eye. "Jehovah seeth not as man seeth; for man looketh on the outward

appearance, but Jehovah looketh on the heart" (1 Sam.
16:7). This is why man's judgment is partial and God's
judgment is complete; ours in biased, His without respect
to persons; man's judgment is often unjust but God's is
according to truth. God judges the Jews according to
the true reality of heart, and not according to their for-
malities in religion. They had a form of godliness, but
their lives denied the power thereof (cf. 2 Tim. 3:5).

2:3

λογίζῃ δὲ τοῦτο (And reasonest thou this). Verse 2 says
we know God judges evil doers according to the inner
realities of the heart. This verse asks, Do you suppose
that thou, thyself, who knows right and practises evil,
can escape God's one and only method of judging, which
is according to truth? You thereby vainly reason that
you will be judged according to what is unreal. You commit Gentile sins and think you will escape their punishment. God must be true; first, to Himself, and also to
you Jews. You, knowing right and practising the contrary—sinning against light—will certainly be involved
in an inescapable judgment. You can not escape the judgment of man, much less can you escape the judgment of
God. You condemn evil through a divine instinct which
is prophetic of the certainty of the awful judgment of
God.

The Jews thought they could escape God's judgment,
because (1) they were hearers of the law (2:13) and (2)
upon the ground that they bore the name "Jew" (2:17,
28, 29) and (3) upon their hereditary favor in being the
descendants of Abraham (Matt. 3:9; 12:11f; John 8:33;
Gal. 2:15).

ὦ ἄνθρωπε (O Man). Paul repeats the generic word
"man" to bring again all Jews into the same guilt and to
one judgment; and at the same time to identify the Jew
and Gentile in the unity of corrupt and condemned humanity (cf. 2:1).

σὺ is the emphatic personal pronoun meaning "thou, thyself."

The word "escape" implies an approaching judgment.

2:4

ἤ (or) holds the question of verse 3 vividly in mind, and at the same time introduces a second question. This little word blockades every avenue of escape and brushes away every excuse, and demands a confession to one question or the other as the only alternative for the Jews. Paul has so taken them that they are forced to confess; either that they expect to escape a righteous judgment for their own sins, or that they despise the mercies and goodness of God. Verse 2 shatters their hope (2:3) of escaping the judgment. Then Paul eliminates and dismisses for them the first dilemma as answered and proven, and convicts them chiefly under the second alternative, which he develops through verse 11.

καταφρονεῖς (despiseth) literally means to think down upon. The important thing in this word is that they "thought." Their "despite" to God's mercy was not excusable through ignorance; neither did it grow out of their not recognizing God's goodness when they saw it. Their reaction grew out of their moral reasoning with reference to His goodness. The word shows intelligence, reasoning, and understanding. They reasoned concerning what they understood to be God's special beneficent goodness, and their conclusions were: that of rebellion towards the Giver, that they merited His favor, and that His favor was not only approval but license. The expression does not mean that they hated His goodness. History and experience show that the Jew loves material blessings. The sin of the Jews, as expressed in this word, is rebellion against the purpose of the divine favors—which purpose is to lead them to repentance and salvation. They did not despise God's favors, but they did despise the purpose of His favors; and hardened their hearts in

impenitence. This is the heart of the word, and is the
attitude of the Jew to the present day.

τοῦ πλούτου τῆς χρηστότητος . . . (the riches of His goodness and forbearance and long-suffering). "Goodness"
denotes positive dealings, while "forbearance and long-
suffering" denote negative dealings, that is, what has not
befallen them, but is justly due them. "The riches of His
goodness" exhausts the idea that God has been all that He
could be to man. And the other two words exhaust the
idea of God's delaying just punishment. Therefore "goodness," as God's positive dealings, and "forbearance and
long-suffering," as His negative dealings, exhaust the
idea of God's merciful dealings with man.

"Goodness" is God's special beneficent favor in contrast to penal justice. "Forbearance" denotes delay in
punishment. "Long-suffering" denotes the patient dura-
tion of time in the "forbearance," and further reveals God
as suffering rather than punishing. "Forbearance" delays
to punish the offense, while "long-suffering" bears and
endures; that is, suffers for the offense rather than the
guilty bearing the punishment for his own sin. In this
word is a foreshadow and intimation of the substitutionary atonement. "Forbearance" will avenge—some day.
The punishment is only delayed and not canceled. But
"long-suffering" is opposed to wrath and revenge, and
would never punish; but would rather bear both the guilt
and the punishment; that is, "long-suffering" would atone
for sin. "Forbearance" must be just, though graciously
delaying the justice; but "long-suffering" would be for-
giving. The first would wait awhile; the second would
wait forever. The one would finally inflict the penalty,
the other would never. The one will end in wrath, the
other changelessly endures. "Forbearance" must win
and inflict the penalty on sin. "Long-suffering" must lose
and give place to wrath. But in the death of Jesus on the
cross, "long-suffering" conquers—atoning for sin by dying. On the cross mercy and justice kissed each other

(cf. Ps. 85:10). Wherefore, God can be just and at the same time justify the unjust (3:26).

εἰς (unto) shows that the purpose of the goodness was to induce to repentance and salvation. God mis-spends His bounty and man misuses it, unless it produces repentance in man. His object is to lead man to the Source of Goodness, to the Storehouse of His bounty, and to the True Substance and Reality of all things (Isa. 1:3). False reasoning with reference to His goodness, and rebellion as their conclusion, rendered them ignorant of God's purpose in blessing them. They knew His goodness; they reasoned concerning it; the erroneous conclusions issued in rebellion; and thereby they willfully failed to come into possession of a true understanding of God's purpose. Regard for His purpose would have led to repentance; but their "thinking down" (despising) led to rebellion against God in His purpose. Their false hope to escape the judgment (2:3) was a further incentive for their ignorance of the divine purpose in mercy, forbearance, and long-suffering.

2:5

κατὰ (according to) denotes cause. The hardness and impenitence is the cause of the wrath. This word also implies justice and equality; the wrath and judgment will be according to, that is, in proportion to the hardness of the impenitent heart.

δὲ (but) contrasts God's purpose (2:4) with what actually happened. This subordinate conjunction emphasizes the breach in how far man fell short of God's expectation; and introduces wrath upon wrath as the antithesis of the salvation with which God wanted, purposed, and labored to bless man. In this word, we can see God's disappointment, hear His sigh from shattered hopes, and feel a new impulse in His heart; but it is purposed for the "day of wrath." κατὰ (according to) preceding δὲ (but) promotes the emphasis and tension of thought rather than leaving it with "God's purpose" in the preceding verse.

σκληρότητά καὶ ἀμετανόητον (hardness and impenitent). Paul expresses hardness and impenitence with adjectives rather than with verbs, because he conceives of the hardness and impenitence, not as acts but as facts; not as process but as accomplished results; not as deeds but as the condition of heart; not calling attention to practice but emphasizing the nature of the heart. God's bounty hardened their hearts when it should have softened them. Their blessing became a curse; their good became their evil; their food became their poison; the more the tree was cultivated and watered, the less fruit it yielded; and plowing only made the field more barren. The hardness grew out of impenitence. Impenitence is the source of hardness. It is not sin that hardens the heart, but impenitence. The heart that will not repent grows harder.

καρδίαν (heart). See the notes on this word in 1:21.

θησαυρίζεις (gathers and lays up, treasurest up). This word woefully pictures the accumulated wrath in contrast to the "riches of His goodness" in verse 4. The present tense shows that the accumulated guilt and wrath has no interruption in their continuous growth. The Jews are to be condemned under accumulated wrath for accumulated sins. Their sins increased, not only in number, but also in volume. Their punishment will be greater than that of the Gentiles; for in addition to their other sins, they have done despite to the fatherly wooings of God's mercy. The meanest of sins are those against mercy, goodness, and love. The wrath of heaven (1:18) condemns the Gentile though he has no special mercy to woo him; then greater shall be the judgment upon the Jew for adding despite to guilt in violating the Father's gracious invitations.

σεαυτῷ (to thyself) convicts and points to man as the party responsible for the wrath; and at the same time, this expression finally defends God against the false notion that it is He who sends men to hell. God takes the initiative in salvation, but man takes the initiative in wrath. Salvation grows out of what God is in Himself, and the judgment grows out of what man is in himself.

2. *God judges according to works.* 2:6-10

2:6

κατὰ τὰ ἔργα αὐτοῦ (according to his works). Paul did not offer any proof for a judgment day, since the Jews accepted this truth as taught by the prophets. But he mentions a second principle or method in the judgment. In verses 2:1-5, he proved that God will judge every one "according to truth"; now (2:6-10), he says God will render to every man "according to his works." There is no incompatibility in these two expressions. "Works" here does not deny the inner realities of heart, as mentioned in other parts of this chapter and Epistle. Neither does this Scripture say that salvation is of works rather than through the unmerited gift of God's grace. This verse is not talking about salvation but judgment in its execution. "According to truth," that is, according to the inward reality of man, is God's method of knowing man for the purpose of execution in the judgment day. "According to works" refers to sin in its external manifestations. The expression is used to humanize the judgment as something tangible instead of abstract, real instead of vague.

The two terms are harmonized in the unity of their meaning. "According to truth" is the subjective reality, and "according to works" is the objective manifestation. The first denotes nature; the second denotes the issues of nature. The first suggests condition; the second suggests practice. The former denotes the presence of sin; the latter denotes the practice of sin. In the one, man is sinful; in the other, man is sinning. In the first, man is being; and in the second, man is doing. What a man is determines what he does; but what he does never makes him what he is. Nature colors action but action never forms nature. The tree is a peach long before it produces peaches. The fruit is determined by the nature of the tree. And the fruit is the same as the nature of the tree. Therefore, the judgment "according to truth" and the judgment "according to works" denote the inner and outer reality of the same thing.

2:8

ἐριθίας (factious) are those who electioneer, who plot to obtain an office, who seek distinctions. The verb means to wrangle, to engage in strife. ἐριθεύω (hireling, paid worker) was used of those paid to campaign, to electioneer, to promote party interests and spirit, to disturb harmony, and to oppose single-mindedness.

ἀπειθοῦσι (disobey) literally means not to be persuaded, not induced by winning words. "Truth" is the revealed will of God—that which ought to be believed and lived. Truth had no persuasive influence over the factious.

In the last part of the verse, Paul states that the wranglers did obey "unrighteousness." ἀδικία (unrighteousness) means immorality (See the same word in 1:18). They were not persuaded by "truth," but were easily persuaded by "immorality." The wranglers were not induced to act according to the fine persuasion of truth; but they never resisted the appeal of immorality. They were rebellious to truth; but were obedient—and more—they were the willing servants of immorality. Both ideas of mind and action are in this word—literally, to be persuaded to act. Immorality dominated their minds and directed their activities. Nothing else made any appeal to their minds, nor formed a motive for their actions. Both truth and immorality have the article. Truth is thereby shown in its clearness and unity. And immorality is personalized as a master who implicitly rules and sways by the slightest suggestions of the impure.

ὀργὴ καὶ θυμός (wrath and indignation). The latter is the climax of the two words. "Wrath" is God's anger held somewhat in subjection, while "indignation" is the occasional outburst in execution. The former is more the disposition, while the latter refers to the manifestation. The first is anger somewhat at rest, the second is anger boiling in all its turbulent fury. The one denotes wrath within; the other denotes wrath as it overflows. The first is like the rumbling of thunder, the second is like the occasional stroke of lightning. The former is the heat of the fire; the latter is the bursting forth of the flames (cf. Wrath, 1:18, and Judgment, 2:2).

2:9

θλίψις καὶ στενοχωρία (tribulation and anguish). These two words denote punishment and suffering. The latter is the stronger word. "Wrath and indignation" is the God-ward side of the punishment, while "tribulation and anguish" is the human side of the suffering. The first two words are cause, and the last two are effect. "Tribulation" refers to the outward infliction, while "anguish" refers to inward suffering. The first denotes objective punishment, while the second denotes subjective torment. The one denotes oppression; the other denotes a conscience that can not rest. These two words exhaust the idea of torment from the wrath of God.

ἐπὶ πᾶσαν ψυχὴν ἀνθρώπου (upon every soul of man). This indicates that it is the soul that is the suffering part of man. This does not mean that the body can not feel. It does mean that all the body can suffer is not to be compared with the torment of soul as it is exposed to the wrath and indignation of the righteous Judge. Punishment will be pre-eminently upon the soul, which feels more keenly, and is the part of man that will suffer most.

κατεργαζομένου (working, working down, exhausting). κατά (down) is used with this word with reference to both good and bad. The prefix strengthens the force of "work," and expresses accomplishment, bringing to pass. They finished their evil work. They carried evil to its consummation. They worked themselves down in evil. They spent their energy and strength in sin. They exhausted themselves in their vices. "Work" in the following verse does not have this prefix.

Ἰουδαίον πρῶτον (to the Jews first). Wrath and indignation together with tribulation and anguish will punish every soul that works evil. Certainly the Gentile will have his rightful place in the judgment, but the Jew will precede the Gentile. In 1:16, Paul accorded the Jew first place in leadership and responsibility. Who shall be first in the judgment but he who defaulted in his responsibility? The person most responsible is most guilty when unfaithful to a trust. Ability brings added responsibility. The Jew is accountable for all that he could have been and is not. The Jew gladly accepted the honor, as Paul accorded first place to him in 1:16. It is self-evident that his being first in leadership and responsibility gives him first place also in the judgment by reason of his failure to discharge known duty.

2:10

Paul startled every Jew by the horror of a worse judgment for them than even the Gentiles deserve. But this verse holds out hope to them and seeks to allure them into duty by stating that the first place in rewards is yet reserved for the Jew, if only he will be faithful in his place of responsibility. This verse indicates that first place in the reward of glory, honor, and peace will just as easily go to the Gentile, when he outstrips the Jew in the righteousness of God. The Jew has no monopoly on first honors in reward, and the Gentile is not underprivileged. This place is for either Jew or Gentile who can meet the requirements (Matt. 20:23). Paul takes up this thought again in chapter 11, and shows how the Jew is some day to take his rightful place in the Christian leadership of the world, to which he is now a defaulting stranger.

3. *God judges without respect of person.* 2:11-15

2:11

"For there is no respect of persons with God." The specific distinction here is the difference between the people

of one nation and those of another. The general distinction is that God does not have judicial regard for any of
the characteristics that aid man in distinguishing one
man from another. Some of these characteristics would
be dress, color, habits, locality, language, nationality,
privilege, possessions, facial distinctions, etc. Every man
is distinct from every other man. He has many characteristics and features that are individual and personal to
him, all of which aid us in distinguishing him from any
other. But God is not limited to human means of making
distinctions. He knows every man, and knows each as
distinct from any other. God transcends our distinctions.
We distinguish men by those things we see externally.
God makes inner distinctions of character without reference to anything external. Man looks at nationality; God
sees nature. Man has respect to fine clothes; God has
respect to the robe of fine linen, pure and clean, which is
the righteousness of the saints (Rev. 19:8, 14). Man regards riches; God regards the riches of His grace as applied to the human heart. Man has respect to the many
colors among the nations; with God there are only two
colors—white and black, that is, good and bad, pure and
vile, saved and lost, redeemed and condemned. Man distinguishes by characteristics; God's distinction is character.

2:12

ὅσοι (as many as) limits the number to less than universal, and holds the statement true to every given case.

The Gentiles sinned without the written law of Moses,
and they will not be judged according to the Mosiac law
nor receive the penalties therein laid down. They are condemned without a written law. Then, under the weight
of what law do they perish? They did not live up to what
law they knew, and are accountable under what law they
have. They perish under the law they possess. They receive only the penalties of the laws they transgress. Just
condemnation is not limited to a knowledge of a written
law. (Deut. 27:26).

Since Gentiles perish for sinning without a written law; then certainly Jews, who sin under the law, shall be judged by the law. They are not licensed to sin under the law. The law does not shield a sinner, nor save the offender, but condemns him. "Perish" was used with reference to Gentiles without law, and "judged" is used in connection with the Jews under the law, because the law is conceived as a definite standard.

2:13

In verse 12, Paul robs the Jews of their ease by saying that the possession of the law will be of no avail in the judgment. In this verse, he says the mere hearing of the law furnishes no safety in the day of wrath.

οὐ οἱ ἀκροαταὶ (not the hearers). The scrolls of the law were scarce and expensive. So the public reading of the Scripture became an important part of their worship. There are many New Testament references to such reading on the Sabbath in the synagogue. Visiting Jews were often called upon for the public reading of the law (Luke 4:16-29).

Hearing the law can not justify. There is no virtue in hearing the law, except as the hearer is transformed, that he might live the law and be free from the law. The law demands and prescribes perfection, but man has transgressed it and is condemned under it. Therefore, if man is saved, he must have freedom from the law; and freedom must come through righteousness—a righteousness other than law-righteousness. This Epistle is written to reveal a grace-righteousness for all, since none have the law-righteousness.

"The doers of the law are just." This does not deny the thesis of the Epistle—a faith-righteousness. If man had never sinned, he would be justified by the law. But man is a sinner both by nature and by practice. And neither Jews with the written law nor Gentiles without law have lived up to the law they have and know. Obedience is not outward to external law, but an inward fellowship of personality with the Personal God. Obedience is not outward to law, but inward harmony to the will of God, and this is the essence of faith. It is the inward harmony that produces the outward obedience. Faith enables a man to do and to obey. Faith, love, and even obedience are inner dispositions of nature, and are never external. Only the expression of them ever becomes external.

<h3 style="text-align:center">2:14</h3>

"Gentile" without the article indicates the number as indefinite. The article would have indicated all Gentiles. The statement to follow is not true of all, but holds good with some.

The article with "law" denotes the written law as given by Moses.

φύσει (nature) denotes the heathen as acting from what is natural to him without external revelation.

ἑαυτοῖς εἰσὶν νόμος (are a law unto themselves). They have a law. The absence of the article holds this law inferior to written law; but nevertheless, law. The Gentiles live by this inner law; they acquit and condemn according to it. The presence of the article here would have made the conscience the whole and only law for the Gentiles. The absence of the article shows their unwritten law to be the written law of Moses, as far as they do it. Therefore, there is only one law. It is partly revealed inwardly to Gentiles, while the Jews have the additional revelation of it in writing. The moral nature in the Gentile takes the place of the written law deposited with the Jew. There is no heathen nation so steeped in sin and ignorance but what has some form of law. It will not be highly organized, and may not be written in their courts. There is no nation so depraved as to reward vice and condemn virtue. No nation puts a premium on murder; no people approve of adultery. These things are illegal even under the crudest of laws. Their worshiping idols shows that religion is also written in their hearts. Therefore, being without the written law does not deprive them of a law—being a law unto themselves—showing that they have in their nature an unwritten law that harmonizes in essence with the written law of Moses. This proves the unity of law, written or imbedded in nature, to have a common source—God the Great Lawgiver. And all men, though in different forms, have the revealed will of God. This heightens the value of the natural law written in the hearts of the Gentiles.

2:15

τὸ ἔργον (the work) being singular emphasizes individual cases rather than a universal rule.

"Heart" is the seat of man's nature, and therefore the source of all his conduct (See the same word in 1:21). Paul is not saying that the law in the hearts will save the Gentiles. He says it will not save. But he says it will come just as near saving him, as the Mosaic law will save the Jews. If the Jew is saved by his law, then the Gentile is also saved, for he has virtually the same.

συνειδήσεως (conscience). Paul pointed to works as the first witness proving the Gentiles to have an inner law. Now he summons their conscience as a second witness. He could not have called a more convincing witness than the conscience, that comforts and torments in doing good and evil respectively. Conscience is the reflective part of man, by which he judges the moral qualities of action—whether his or another's.

συνμαρτυρούσης (witness together with). The prefix (with, together with) denotes conscience as agreeing with work, that is, the internal testimony and the external evidence corroborate.

Then the Apostle summons a third witness—their mutual thoughts. Their moral judgment with reference to a given act takes one of two alternatives: it accuses or excuses. "Accusing or excusing" shows that the natural law written in the Gentile conscience has standards for human conduct, by which they acquit and condemn.

The Gentiles have a moral law inwardly written in their hearts.

(1) This partial conformance to the written law of Moses is evidence that they have a law—written in their hearts.
(2) The conscience either reproaches or approves personal acts.
(3) The thought mutually held and reciprocally exchanged reveals a standard of moral values whereby they judge—(a) accusing or condemning, or (b) excusing and acquitting.

4. *God judges according to Paul's gospel.* 2:16

2:16

τὰ χρυπτὰ means covered ways, vaults, cellars. It is the vault that is mentioned, but it is the concealed things in the vault to which reference is made. The force of the picture is that the vault will be no protection to the hidden treasures of sin. These things are more than hid —they are jealously guarded and secretly protected. The hidden sins in concealed vaults are the ones most valued— the valuables of life, the treasures of the heart, of a lost person! These are the secrets that sinners feel are safe from any eye, judgment, or penalty. The emphasis is that since God knows the hidden lives of men secretly protected in concealed vaults, He certainly knows the vile sins of open rebellion. "In the day" has the force of "in that day," God shall raid the cellars, plunder the vaults, disclose the hidden, and reveal the secret things of life—for judgment. Nothing is concealed before His all-seeing and all-searching eye; nor is there any protection for the treasured cellars in the day of judgment.

The Jews thought they would be judged by the law; but Paul says Christ is the Judge, and that the gospel is the standard. The gospel is the revelation of the righteousness of God in Jesus Christ. God's righteousness, as revealed in the gospel, is the standard, and the law is the executioner or condemning agent in the judgment. The law was never the standard of life. He who seeks only to meet the requirements of the law, has a low standard. The law promises death and never promised life. The reverse is not in the power of the law. The law was given to convict and not to convert. It proclaims guilt but has no cleansing power. Law must be just and never justify; the law convicts but can not forgive. The law lashes and leaves bleeding but it can not heal the stripes.

τὸ εὐαγγέλιόν μου (my gospel) refers to the faith-righteousness as opposed to the unknown law-righteousness. Paul's gospel is that of grace to even the uncircumcised Gentile. His gospel is a new law for both Jew and Gentile, enabling them to keep both the Mosaic law and that written in the conscience of man. "My gospel" distinguishes the faith-righteousness from all the doctrines of the false teachers. And this faith-righteousness is the sole standard in the judgment. Those without faith will have no righteousness, and they shall meet the law—only in execution.

5. *God judges according to light.* 2:17-25

2:17

σὺ (thou) here identifies the Jew as the defenseless "man" in 2:1, and as the condemned victim before the inescapable and approaching judgment in 2:3. σὺ (thou) here also names the Jew as the person to whom the personal and familiar pronouns σου (thy) and σεαυτῷ (thyself) refer in 2:5; and thus points to the Jew as "thou art the man," whose "hardness and impenitent heart treasurest up for thyself wrath in the day of wrath and revelation of the righteous judgment" (2:5).

Ἰουδαῖος (Jew) is the national name for God's people, and it distinguishes them from all other nations, that is, from the heathen. Their name denotes them as the Chosen People of God. This title denotes a people, whose history is a record of God's dealings with man.

ἐπονομάζῃ (bearest a name, named upon, named in addition to). ἐπὶ (upon) denotes the name as superior to any other national name. The prefix thereby ranks the Jew as first among the nations of the earth. Thus, the title is the most honorable, and those bearing it should be the most honorable; and since it is the most honorable name among the nations, those bearing it should live so that it would be honored by the nations, and finally among the nations. The passive voice (thou hast been named) denotes the name as given rather than as received; thus referring the name, Jew, to divine origin. Herein lies the chief honor attached to the name. And it should lead the Jew to honor and reverence instead of to shame and blasphemy. The subjunctive mood convicts them as not living up to the excellency of the name; and indicates that they live so far beneath its significance that it ceases to be really their name; and thereby, not only defaming them, but "denaming" them, and leaving them disowned and disinherited without a name.

ἐπ-ανα-παύῃ (restest upon). The Jew rests, supports, lies, leans, reclines upon the law for the assurance of salvation. The verb part means to restrain, to cease, to leave off. Their rest was not a peaceful trust in the law, but a cessation which was equivalent to violation. They did not trust to the law, they relaxed on the law. This cessation was not keeping of the law but the violation of the law. This is a false trust, as is indicated by the subjunctive mood. It is a stupefied peace that will be aroused by eternal torment.

The absence of the article from law indicates that the whole of law is not in the mind of the Apostle. This convicts the Jew of trusting to only a portion of the law and ignoring the remainder. Thus, he has false hope in a portion and ignores the remainder, and is thereby a transgressor of the whole law.

καυχᾶσαι ἐν θεῷ (boasteth in God). Both the word and the middle voice refer to selfish boasting rather than righteous glorying toward God. They boasted in themselves that they were rightfully God's, instead of glorifying God that He was righteously theirs. The boasting grew out of pride and not out of gratitude. It was the boasting of the tongue and not the glorying of the heart.

The absence of the article from "God" indicates that they boasted themselves with reference to His deity, but not with reference to His Person. They gloried in a system of divinity but not in a Person. Their boasting was not directed towards a Person and therefore did not find the divine personal response. They boasted about God but did not glorify Him. They knew about Him but did not know Him. They prayed about Him but did not pray to Him. They performed with reference to Him but they did not live Him.

This last clause is the climax of the three statements in this verse.

2:18

τὸ θέλημα (the will) having the article denotes God's will as clearly revealed, well understood, unified, not indefinite, nor poorly revealed. γινώσκεις (know by experience) further reveals that they knew inwardly in their hearts what was God's will. The emphasis from the article denotes full well that God's will is mentioned here, and not another's. The presence of the article gives individuality to this "will," as being pre-eminently above all other wills. The pre-eminence of this will is so indicated as to denote its being the one will, the whole will, the only will, and the sovereign will. This is to be man's one guide, his whole guide, and his only guide. No other will is to have dominion over man's will and conscience. No human will has a right to assume any authority over another's in matters of conscience and religion.

And no human can serve, as some freely but falsely claim, as mediator between the will of man and the divine will; nor can a human being interpose between the free fellowship and communion of another's will and that of the Infinite. The revelation, fellowship, and obedience of God's will is and must be a personal response of will unto will and personality to personality. Only God has the

right of dominion over the mind, the will, and the conscience of man.   But even God will not violate the freedom of the human will in its right of contrary choice.

κατηχούμενος (being instructed, being instructed orally,
being sounded down upon).   They sounded out the law
orally and didactically in the synagogues.   They sounded
down upon doctrine.   They were well instructed.   κατὰ
(down) shows thoroughness. Thus, they knew the will of
God, and discriminated in favor of the excellent.

τοῦ νόμου (the law).   Law having the article indicates
that they were taught the whole law, though they rested
upon only a portion of it (2:17).

2:19-20

The blind, the wayward, the foolish, the babes are not
the Gentiles, as some write.   They are rather the mass of
the Jews, that is, the unofficial Jews.   The Jews never felt
it their duty nor made it their office to teach the Scripture
to the blind, foolish, ignorant Gentiles.   Paul's reprimand
here is not to the Jew in general, but to Jews in high
places, the official Jews, the priests, scribes, teachers,
doctors, those who teach the masses.   They rightly teach
the masses because of their ability and superior knowledge of the law.   The masses are as babes in comparison
to these trained teachers.

In these high places was where Judaism culminated.
And here Paul attacks them as the most corrupt in the
most vital places of responsibility and leadership.   Paul
follows Micah's example, as he convicted those in high
places in Samaria and Jerusalem (1:5).   Too often the
worst corruption lies with those who ought to be the best;
and the breakdown comes from those who profess moral
support.   The conviction of the corrupt officials does not
justify the masses as innocent.   Since the head is so sick,
what must be the condition of the whole body!   Since the
best is so corrupt, what must be the pollution of the un-
leavened masses!   Since the teacher can not learn his

own lesson, there is no hope for the pupils. Since the guide is already lost, how shall the blind find his way! The corrector of the foolish must not be the biggest fool. The correction of the foolish will not correct, but will only irritate when the corrector is only another fool—and a bigger fool.

μόρφωσιν (form) refers to the external appearance. Knowledge and truth took concrete form and shape in the written law.

2:21-22

οὐ (not) demands an affirmative answer, and forces them to admit that they do not teach themselves what they teach others, that is, they do not learn what they teach; and they break the laws they enforce on others. The Jews must admit that they have failed to learn the lessons that they seek to teach to others.

"Do you steal? Do you commit adultery? Do you rob temples?" Paul used the repeated present tense in asking these questions. This tense describes action as recurring at successive intervals. He questions even to the occasional action: "Do you ever steal? Do you ever commit adultery? Do you ever rob temples?" Their conduct contradicted their instructions to the masses. They taught a better way than they lived.

βδελυσσόμενος (abhorring idols). The abhorring carries the idea of physical repulsion and bodily shrinking in horror from idols. Paul climaxes the crimes of the official Jew with temple-plundering and idol-pillage. The Jew professed to abhor idols, but he liked to plunder heathen shrines (cf. Josephus, Antiquities, 4:8, 10). This is the most striking contrast between what Jews taught and what they practiced. They revealed their inability for making moral discriminations, when they failed to distinguish between the horror of idols and the committing of sacrilege. The Jews can not clear themselves of sacrilege in Gentile eyes, when they plunder and steal the temple gold that is held sacred to the idolatrous Gentile.

2:23

"Who gloriest in the law." Interpret this phrase in the light of the exegesis of "gloriest in God" in 2:17.

"Through thy transgression of the law, thou dishonorest God." The present indicative so convicts the transgressors, that this clause should not be regarded as a question. This is the mildest and yet the most convicting way of summing up the aforementioned sins of the teachers, guides, and correctors. The Jews are dishonored in their sins, but God's honor is involved more. The highest glory from man's salvation is that God's name is glorified (cf. 1:5). Likewise, transgression leaves its worst stain on the honor of God.

They boasted themselves in the law, and at the same time lived on low plains. They did not seek to live above the law as free men, but forced and twisted the law to justify their sinful lives. They boasted in the law, but their transgressions showed only contempt for the character that is expressed in the law. The transgression showed that their glorying in the law was only empty boasting. If the glorying had been from the heart, they would have surrendered their lives to have been governed by the law; but men, whose praise is of the tongue, transgress from the heart. The tongue is not the governing principle of life; but out of the heart come the issues of life (Prov. 4:23).

Transgression is not merely violation of God's law; it is rebellion of personality against the moral character of God. Law is the character of God objectified. Law is the expression of God's essence, moral nature, personality, and heart. Transgression of law is the expression of the same on the part of the sinner. Violation of law is transgression of heart against heart, rebellion of personality against personality, collision of natures. Violation of law is infidelity, seeking to strike a death blow at the very existence of God. Transgression of law is rebellion and hatred, in defiance of personality. Lawlessness is wickedness and corruption attacking the moral nature of

God. Obedience is the moral response of the heart of man to the moral nature of the heart of God.

2:24

"For the name of God is blasphemed among the Gentiles because of you, as it is written." (cf. Isa. 52:5). The only visible result from the Jews' knowledge and teaching of the Scripture was that Jehovah was blasphemed among the Gentiles. Immoral Jewish conduct gave the impression to the Gentiles that they had a wicked and immoral God. The wicked Gentile was consistent in his immorality, for his deities practiced the same things and enjoined such upon him as acts of duty even in religious services (cf. 1:23). Out of such a background, the Gentile reasoned that Jehovah was immoral and lawless before the Jews. The Gentile practiced only those things enjoined by their deities, and therefore concluded that the Jewish immorality and lawlessness were acts of worship or in harmony with their God—Jehovah. This does not mean that the Gentile was better than the Jew, but he was more consistent than the Jew. When the Gentile wanted to practice some sin, he found and worshipped a god who practiced, approved, and even enjoined such a practice; or he found the new practice in a present god. The heathen and immoral Gentile did only those things in which their deities could participate; while the Jew lived in open rebellion and defiance to the revealed will of God and did that which dishonored God. This is a woeful commentary on the lives of some so-called Christians, who can carry God neither into their society nor their business.

The above questions about theft, adultery, and temple-robbery grew out of the fact that the Jews had caused the Gentiles to blaspheme Jehovah.

"As it is written," coming at the close of a quotation, is unusual and contrary to practice. The placing of it before the quotation is the right method for giving proper recognition for a quotation. Here it would seem that Paul almost forgot to give credit to Isaiah. The reason for this setting is that Paul is not only calling up a prophetic Scripture to prove his point; but is discussing an historical fact which was true in Isaiah's day. The emphasis is not that the blasphemy is fulfilled, but that the blashphemy is no new thing, having been true in Isaiah's day even as he recorded (52:5). The emphasis is not upon its being the fulfillment of prophecy, but upon its continuous existence, even from the day of Isaiah's record in prophecy. The quotation is not a proof text, but indicates how long the blasphemy has existed. Paul is not trying to prove that the Gentiles blaspheme God, but is showing how long they have blasphemed Him because of Jewish immorality. The expression is truly Paul's. It is only a statement of what was actually occuring at the time Paul was writing—and it coincides with Scripture. "As it is written" seems to be an afterthought with Paul, to say, "My accusation is founded upon Scripture as well as observation."

2:25

Circumcision is the seal of righteousness by faith, as will be shown in the fourth chapter of this Epistle. Circumcision is profitable if you have that for which it is the sign. But the Jew could not derive profit from the bare sign. The seal to be valid, required faith. The sign without the faith is just as worthless as the brand without the animal, or as a dollar mark without the cash.

"A doer of the law" does not teach salvation by works. Rather Paul is teaching the contrary. Circumcision is profitable if you keep the law. And the first thing the law requires, with reference to circumcision, is that faith shall be the substance of the seal. Then faith enables a man to keep the law in Christ. He is a doer of the law because he has saving faith. Thus, circumcision has a meaning. Faith is the value, circumcision is an interpretation of that value. Faith is the substance, circumcision is the shadow. The first is the reality, while the second is the sign. The one brings salvation, the other is the profession.

The former brings the redemption, the latter is the evidence. The one obtains the promise, while the latter is the testimony of His immutability.

Circumcision is uncircumcision, unless it be inward, of the heart. "Uncircumcision" in this verse is without the article, and denotes Gentile character, that is, unregenerate nature.

6. *God judges according to the heart.* 2:26-29

2:26

The "uncircumcision" refers to the Gentiles. Paul is not saying that the uncircumcised can be saved by keeping the law, any more than law will save the circumcision. He is saying that a moral Gentile without circumcision excells the immoral Jew with circumcision; and that righteousness without the sign would be better than the sign without the righteousness. The next verse says the contrast will be condemning to the Jew. And 1:18-32 is Paul's commentary on Gentile guilt and condemnation.

"Law" has the article. This marks the case as hypothetical; and states the impossibility of salvation by law. The article indicates that the whole law must be kept—no exception, no substitution, no falling short, no mercy, but absolute exaction. No son of Adam could keep the law because he is inherently lawless.

2:27

"Judge" is emphatic by its position. The Jew has no moral advantage over the Gentile. Rather the Gentile example will put the Jew to shame. The uncircumcised Gentile without the written law performs some acts by nature. Thus, the Gentile does better from nature than the Jew does by aid of revelation. For the Gentile does not have the law, and yet complies with some of it; while the Jew has all the law written, and yet complies with none of it but breaks all of it.

The article with "law" shows the case to be still hypothetical, as the whole law can not be performed by even one Gentile (cf. "law" in 2:26). Paul's purpose is to show the Jews' condition to be no better than that of the Gentiles'. To do this, he shows that the Jew sinned against more light than the Gentile, and therefore is involved in more guilt and greater condemnation.

2:28

Being a Jew is an inward matter of the spirit. It is the work of God in the nature of the soul. External things do not make a man a Jew. "Jew" is here used to denote God's people. Profession, dress, ceremonial service, circumcision, church membership, and baptism do not constitute divine ownership. Natural descent guarantees only inherent sins. Being a son of Abraham (Matt. 3:9) does not make the Jew a child of God. Abraham is not divine, but obtained sonship through faith. Faith is the internal counterpart of the external sign. Circumcision is uncircumcision, if it is only outward. If the nature is unchanged, the sign is not only vain but hypocritical. (See the notes on "truth" in 2:2; cf. 2:11).

2:29

"He is a Jew who is one inwardly." Abrahamic descent is to be traced inwardly. He is the father of the faithful —the believers. Descent from him is a matter of faith; it is a spiritual descent. A genealogy from Abraham does not prove spiritual sonship. But faith makes the believer, whether Jew or Gentile, an immediate son of Abraham. Genealogy makes the Jew a far distant grandson of Abraham; but faith makes the believer a son of Abraham and heir to the promise.

κρυπτῷ (secret things, inwardly) is a neuter noun in the lative case. (See the notes on its cognate in 2:16). This refers to the things in the cellar. The Jew must be one clear down in the cellar and in all the vault—no reservation. He must be a Jew in all the recesses of the inner life. The Christian's life must be open, unquestionable, public to all the people, and above reproach. And God must have access into all the inner chambers of the Christian's heart and life.

καρδίας (of heart) is contrasted from σαρκὶ (flesh) in the preceding verse. σαρκὶ (flesh) denotes unregenerate human nature. It here corresponds to "uncircumcision" in 2:25, which there denoted "Gentile character," and "Gentile character" denotes unrestricted sinful nature. Circumcision is not valid when the nature of the candidate is unregenerate, inherently sinful, and thus identical with Gentile character. Circumcision is inward, of the heart. It is the cutting away of the unclean, impure, corruptible, and sinful nature. Sin has its source in the sinful, fallen nature of man, and must be eradicated from the root. Sin must be cut off at the root, instead of attempting to do it by clipping the bud. Sin must be uprooted and not pruned. Nature must be changed rather than whitewashed. The heart must be cleansed for salvation rather than the body. Human nature must be circumcised rather than the foreskin. It is the heart that must be circumcised (Lev. 26:41; Deut. 10:16; 30:6; Jer. 9:26; Ezek. 44:7; Col. 2:11; Acts 7:51). The uncircumcised heart is the impenitent heart in 2:5.

"Inward," "heart," and "spirit" characterize and designate true circumcision. These are the marks whereby men shall know valid circumcision. "Outward," "of the flesh," "mere letter of law" are the characteristics of counterfeit circumcision, and are the hypocritical marks of unregenerate human nature. Thus, God distinguishes for the world between the true and the false. The true way is inward, of the heart; the false is outward, of the flesh. The one is salvation by grace, the other is salvation by works. The first is of the Lord, the second is of man. The former would give God the praise, the latter would retain the glory for self. The one is a gift from

God, the other is a work of man. The first is wrought in
the nature of man, the second upon his body. The former reaches the source of the trouble, the latter deals only
with pretense. The one is all-sufficient for the insufficient
Gentile, the other is insufficient for the "all-sufficient"
Jew.

ἐν πνεύματι οὐ γράμματι (in the spirit and not in the letter)
are the next two words that are contrasted. They stand
in extreme opposition to one another. "Spirit" can not
mean either the spirit of man or the Holy Spirit as some
erroneously suppose. These two words denote the true
and false nature of circumcision respectively. The "spirit" is the spiritual significance of circumcision; the "letter" is the outward ceremonial act without meaning.
Value resides in the one, meaning is denied the other.
These two words are a further development of the same
ideas above expressed in true circumcision and circumcision that is not circumcision (2:25) ; a Jew that is one
inwardly and another who is so only outwardly; circumcision of the heart and that which is outwardly of the
flesh. Circumcision of the "spirit" corresponds to that of
the heart, while curcumcision of "letter" refers to the
literal mark in the flesh. Paul is pleading for circumcision
in the spirit of the law rather than according to the mere
letter of the law. The letter of a law may be met entirely
by a heart that is in utter rebellion to the spirit of the
law. Valid circumcision is in the spirit of the law, and
not in the letter of the law.

ἐξ (out of) and ἐκ (from) respectively deny man as
the author of this inward grace and attribute all the
glory to God, Who alone can save. The praise for heart
religion is not "out of" man, but "from" God. Grace
robs man of all merit and refers all the glory to God. All
that contributes to man's salvation, God chooses to place
to His own account. "Salvation is of the Lord" (Jonah
2:9), and not of man.

III. WITH OR WITHOUT THE LAW, ALL ARE CONDEMNED

3:1-20

1. Objections anticipated and answered. 3:1-8.

1. Question.	What advantage hath the Jew? 3:1.
Answer.	The Jew has the advantage in every respect, but pre-eminently in being entrusted with the Scriptures. 3:2.
2. Question.	Has the unfaithfulness of the Jews annulled God's purpose? 3:3.
Answer.	Man's unbelief can not make God untrue to His promises. The contrast magnifies God's faithfulness. 3:4.
3. Question.	Then is not the Jew's unrighteousness become a virtue, in that it exhibits God's righteousness? And is not God wrong in punishing the Jew for acts that establish His righteousness? 3:5.
Answer.	Then there would not be any judgment for Jew or Gentile, and sin would become a virtue in man, and the chief glory towards God. And the Jew would be joining in with the Gentile in blaspheming by saying, "Let us do evil that good may come." 3:6ff.

2. The universal corruption of man. 3:9-18.

1. The state of sin in character. 3:9-12.
   (1) The unrighteous denote ill-relation to God. 3:10.
   (2) Inability to give moral and spiritual discrimination. 3:11a.
   (3) They neither recognize nor seek Him. 3:11b.
   (4) Universality of corruption. 3:12a.
   (5) God does not value the corrupt. 3:12b.
   (6) Sin so ill-relates man from God that he can neither live nor serve in the higher relationships of life. 3:12c.

2. The practice of sin in words. 3:13-14.
   (1) Vulgarity: throat an open grave. 3:13a.
   (2) Hypocrisy: they have used deceit with the tongue. 3:13b.
   (3) Slander: poison of asps under lips. 3:13c.
   (4) Profanity: cursing and bitterness. 3:14.

3. The practice of sin in deeds. 3:15-17.
   (1) Crime: swift to shed blood. 3:15.
   (2) Failure: ruin and wretchedness. 3:16.
   (3) Strife: internal and external—the way of peace have they not known. 3:17.

4. The sinful source of the whole. 3:18.
  (1) Reverence is the mother of virtue.
  (2) Irreverence is the mother of vice.

3. The above Old Testament quotations were made against the Jews in that they have the law. 3:19-20.
  1. The law brings universal condemnation. 3:19.
  2. The law can not justify. 3:20a.
  3. The law brings the knowledge of sin. 3:20b.

1. *Objections anticipated and answered.* 3:1-8

3:1

τί οὖν (what then). Paul anticipates objections in the minds of his readers, and by joining in with the objector in asking the question he is able to carry him more safely through the answer. Thus, Paul makes use of a very fine point of psychology by answering the objection before it has become a part of the person who might object. Paul perhaps brings up objections that some reader would not have seen, which only shows Paul to be fair to the opposition and at the same time to be a master of his own proposition. The objections are raised as much for an explanation to the devotee, as they are for the convincing of the unbeliever in the opposition.

"What is the advantage of being a Jew," since he is even more woefully condemned than a Gentile? If the Jew is not saved but lost, and awaiting a heavier judgment than the Gentile, then would it not be better to be a Gentile? Then being a Jew is not a blessing but a curse? Did not God make the distinction? Is He wrong? Do not God's distinctions distinguish? We might ask what is the advantage of being born in a Christian land? Ultimately none, if you do not trust Christ for salvation. Immediately, you have every advantage—to lead you to Christ, and your judgment will be the more severe if your advantages fail.

Paul wiped out the distinction between the circumcision and uncircumcision, condemned outward circumcision as no better than unrestrained Gentile depravity, and exalted circumcision of the heart above literal circumcision of the flesh. He then brings forward the anticipated objection: "What is the profit of circumcision?" None, if you have not the faith for which the circumcision is the sign. But circumcision is rich in advantages favorable to your obtaining the righteousness of God by faith. Circumcision was designed as a monument to faith and not as a stumbling block for unbelief. Circumcision was given to lead to faith and not to be substituted for faith.

3:2

"Much every way." The advantages and profits are not named in this expression, but the absence of the article from πάντα (all) denotes profit from any point considered. This does not denote a particular advantage, but attributes profit to the Jew in every respect considered, though Paul discusses only one of these many values. There is no relationship of life but what is enhanced by being a Jew. Being a Jew is a distinction and a blessing from any point of comparison. In every point, the Jew is placed in advance of the Gentile. In every expression of God to mankind, the Jew has received the better part. In every manifestation of divine interest, the Jew has been the recipient of the more eager portion. The intensity of all God's dealings has been centered upon the Jew. God has literally lived with the Jew—hoping to live in him and through him.

πρῶτον (first). There has been much discussion as to whether Paul meant "pre-eminently and chiefly," or whether he named one advantage and never returned to enumerate the second, third, and others. Paul names the first of a long series of advantages. And he heads the list with the pre-eminent advantage, to denote that others followed without being named. He leaves off the enumeration after naming the first one, for the one named is not only pre-eminent but sufficient for his purpose here, and is really inclusive of every other. Though he does name others in 9:4f.

τὰ λόγια τοῦ θεοῦ (the oracles of the God). The oracles denote the whole of the Old Testament Scriptures, and not any portion. The article with "oracles" denotes unity, the whole, no omission of any part. The genitive of "God" denotes possession; hence, the author, the source. The Scriptures therefore came by inspiration. The article with "God" denotes personality. This at once enhances the value of the Scriptures, and is at the same time a warning and a dread to those in whom the oracles have not been permitted to perform their divine commission. God intrusted the oracles to the Jews, deposited the Scriptures with them, and more—He made promises to them.

ἐπιστεύθησαν (intrusted, "infaithed"). The aorist tense denotes the Scriptures, as being intrusted once for all time to the Jews. The ninth chapter of this Epistle shows that the aorist is correct, and that the Jews are His ultimate hope though they are, for a time, unfaithful. God has no other plan, no other purpose, and no other reservation than that the Jew should be the spiritual leader in the preaching of the Scriptures. He depended upon the faithfulness of the Jews. In the word "intrusted," literally, "infaithed," you can hear a sigh of disappointment, you can feel a broken impulse from betrayed trust, you can see a marred expression from shattered hopes. God trusted the Jews but they did not prove worthy. He "infaithed" them but they did not "infaith" Him. The word of God was intrusted, faithfully deposited, given in divine faith; and it is hereby concluded that His word must in like manner be accepted through faith. The word "intrusted" or "infaithed" reveals God as giving His word, so as to be an everlasting example to man that he is saved by grace through faith.

Two questions were asked in verse one, and only one answer is given in verse two. But that reply is the answer to both questions. The first and inclusive advantage in being a Jew is the possession of the oracles of God. The first and chief profit of circumcision is the possession of the Scriptures as the way of true life. Being a Jew and being circumcised are co-ordinate in the Jewish mind. He thinks circumcision makes him a Jew. So the two questions can be co-ordinated and given one and the same answer. The Scriptures can be given as the answer to almost any question concerning values, advantages, opportunities, privileges, relationships in this life, and the life to be.

3:3

The second objection to be answered is: Has the unfaithfulness of the Jews annulled God's promises?

εἰ ἠπίστησάν τινες (if some were without faith). Paul says some were faithless. The number is vague and indefinite. The term denotes neither few nor many. The trend of the Epistle would indicate many. But Paul says "some" to avoid being offensive, and to deny the universality of unbelief.

μὴ ἡ ἀπιστία αὐτῶν (shall not their unbelief). The double negative is permissible in Greek, and is here emphatic of their lack of faith. ἀπιστία means unbelief, lack of faith, faithless, without faith, no faith, and does not mean unfaithfulness. This word means "unbelief" without exception, unless it might be in 2 Tim. 2:13. "By their unbelief they were broken off; and thou standest by thy faith" (11:20). "And we see that they were not able to enter in (to the Promised Land) because of unbelief" (Heb. 3:19).

Some are inclined to translate ἀπιστία (unbelief) "unrighteousness" instead of "unbelief"; because it is used synonymously with "unrighteousness." The two terms being synonymous is why Paul makes the comparison. The terms "unbelief" and "unrighteousness" (or immorality) are synonymous. Unbelief is immoral. They are the inner reality and external expression of one thing. "Unbelief" is the nature; while "unrighteousness," or "immorality" is the expression of nature. The one is the man, the other is his work. The first is the man concealed to human eyes, the second is the man revealed to human eyes. The former is what a man is, the second is what he does. Unbelief is not non-moral, it is immoral.

Unbelief is not a negative attitude, it is a positive and wicked activity. Unbelief does not lead to immorality, it is immorality.

καταργήσει. This word literally means to "work down." It further means to render inactive, to render invalid, to paralyze, to make powerless, to abolish, to become void, to exhaust.

τὴν πίστιν τοῦ θεοῦ (the faith of God). The "faith" of God is contrasted from the "unbelief" on the part of man. The "infaithing" of the oracles is in apposition to "the faith" of God. The "oracles of God" are given in the "faith of God." "The faith of God" is the assurance of the "promises of God." Therefore, God is able to fulfill all that He has promised. His promise is given and grounded in His immutability.

God promised Israel a Messiah to reign from everlasting unto everlasting in an eternal reign. Will the "unbelief of some" abolish God's promise to Israel? The emphasis is not "will it inabilitate God," but "will there be any one to whom God may be faithful in carrying out His promise." Does not man's forfeiture paralyze God's promise? Does not man's unbelief render God's faith barren and sterile? No! Man's unbelief is no strain on God's faith. God is not dependent upon man for His truthfulness. Unbelief in man will not produce the same in God. God's faith does not degenerate into man's unbelief. The fulfilling of His promises does not depend on the Jews. He could turn to the Gentile; besides there is yet a remnant in Israel. There is yet a live root in Israel into which the Gentiles can be grafted and receive Israel's promise. The unbelief of some can not thwart God's eternal purpose. He will take one in faith and grow a new race. He has cast off His people before, as seen in the selection of Noah and Abraham. He can cast them off again in favor of the Gentiles. God is not dependent upon any person nor group of people. There are some that He would rather use, some He would rather have; but He can raise up a new people to do His will, and to receive His promises, and to inherit the kingdom. God wanted to evangelize the world with Jews; but He was not limited to their faith nor limited by their unbelief. He would like to evangelize the world with Gentiles; but the Gentile is not His last and only resort—there is yet a stump, a seed, a remnant, a hope in Israel.

Israel will some day be restored and God's promises will ultimately be consummated in her.

3:4

μὴ γένοιτο (God forbid), literally, let it not come to pass. This term expresses horror. It is the strongest denial. The emphasis of its denial is not upon some falsehood, but upon the blasphemy and the irreverence expressed by such a view; that is, the expression marks a statement as false primarily because it is blasphemous. And in the term is an apology for even having mentioned the irreverent, and for the conversation having so degenerated.

ἀληθής (true) denotes the immutability of God in keeping His promises.

ψεύστης (liar) denotes man's unbelief in its final issue with reference to the promises of God. Man's unbelief denies God's promises. The promises of God are not fulfilled in man. Man is living with reference to the promises as if God were false. His profession makes God a liar. Paul says God is true, and that it is man who is false. "Liar" refers to the unfulfilled promises; and man is branded a "liar" because it is in him that the promises failed. The unbeliever is a liar (cf. John 5:10); while "the truth of God" (3:4) and "the faith of God" (3:3) are co-ordinate.

Faith is the essential element in any virtue. Man can not be true to facts, to himself, to others, nor to God without faith. Faith is essential to truth, to wisdom, and to a knowledge of God. Those who know the truth must first be the truth. The folly of the world lies in its unbelief. Unbelief is not connected with ignorance but with lying, the perverting of the truth, the refusal of God. Faith is not opposed to knowledge, it is the basis of knowledge, the realm of wisdom, and the evidence. Faith is not the blind acceptance of what you can not understand nor prove; faith is the proof, the way to know. Faith is the intelligent response to the God of truth.

"That thou mightest be justified in thy words, and mightest prevail when thou comest into judgment" (cf. Ps. 51:4). David says his sins give added evidence of God's righteous judgment. His guilt exhibits God's justice. His sins commend the righteousness of God.

3:5

The third objection to be answered is: Then does not the unrighteousness of the Jews become a virtue in that it exhibits God's righteousness; and is not God wrong in punishing the Jews for acts that establish His righteousness?

συνίστησιν (commendeth) means to bring together, to introduce to one another, to recommend, to commend, to prove, to establish.

ἀδικία ἡμῶν (our unrighteousness) is used as a synonym for "unbelief" (cf. unbelief in 3:3), and stands in relation to "every man a liar" in 3:4.

μὴ ἄδικος ὁ θεὸς (is not God unrighteous). The double negative is an emphatic denial of the question that God is unrighteous. μὴ (not), not only expects, but demands a negative answer.

τὴν ὀργήν (the wrath). The article denotes a definite wrath, a consummated wrath, a definite judgment.

The average Jew would have been happy to have shielded his sins with a false pretense that divine glory issued from them. The sinner would rejoice to comfort himself in God's inconsistency in punishing man for producing the glory that He expects to emanate from man. Sin reasons: God would be unrighteous to be offended by His own requirements, and to condemn for the glory He demands.

κατὰ ἄνθρωπον λέγω (I speak according to man). Paul uses this expression as an apology for even discussing a thing so contrary to truth and the nature of God. This expression is inserted lest the reader should carelessly identify Paul with the false doctrine. It bespeaks Paul's horror from such irreverent and impious questioning concerning God's eternal holiness. He infers that he speaks, not as one who knows, but talks as the average Jew would impiously reason. The term used for man is generic, man in common, man in general, man as a whole, man as representative. Thus, he convicts the representative Jew as being guilty of the sin involved in this question. (See note on "man" in 2:1).

3:6

Paul does not answer this blasphemy with a denial. He first expresses his abhorance in verse 5 by saying the language is expressive of collective man ($\mathring{a}\nu\theta\rho\omega\pi o\nu$). And he opens this verse with his usual expression of horror— God forbid (See the same expression in 3:4). Paul's refusal to deny the objection emphasized the question as one that never should have been asked. He therefore concludes that it should not be answered, and that such an impious discussion should not be heard.

Then Paul gives an argument by way of a positive statement. He states the office of God, as the Jews held it in common with him. He states the office of God as Judge of the universe. If the impious objector in verse five were correct, then the judgment of sin would be converted into an occasion to reward all sins. The judgment would be wrecked, and the moral order of the universe would become chaos. The Gentiles would not be punished, and their idolatry could only be rewarded, in that it exhibits more perfectly the true God and commends the worship of the same. And there would be no Judge and no judgment, for there would be no sin. All would be virtue; and no one would have to be righteous to be good. The person in the wrong would be right; the immoral one would be unto God's glory; and God would be unjust when He judges righteously.

3:7

Paul used the first person here so as not to offend (cf. 1 Cor. 4: 6). The "lie" refers back to "liar" in 3:4.

3:8

The Apostle does not seek to answer his question, except to say that condemnation will be just for those who thus reason. Paul does not attack the slanderous report. But why not do evil when it abounds unto glory? If good come from sin, then the more we sin the greater the good. But good never comes from evil. Sin can not glorify God. Sin is not another way to do right. He who sins, never does it to the glory of God. Sin is never committed in honor of the Lord but to dishonor Him. Sin is open rebellion of God. There is never any good in sin and no glory ever came out of sin. But God sometimes makes sin serve the good and forces evil to enhance his glory. In the wisdom of God, He is able somewhat to over-ride the evil design of sin, to check its wicked purposes, and to make it serve his purpose in the way of contrast, warning, and punishment. This is not the highest good, nor the brightest glory. God can not get the good and glory from man's evil that He would from righteousness. All the good that He can get from sin is to reduce its influence to the minimum, over-rule it to some divine intent, and punish the sinner. Therefore, any such good can not be credited to our sins, but to the over-ruling power of the Omniscient God. The good is God's, together with the glory in thus perverting evil; and to man remains only sin, guilt, and punishment.

"Whose condemnation is just." Condemnation in the judgment shall be just for those who reason that God is glorified by their sins, and who "do evil that good may come."

2. *The universal corruption of man.* 3:9-18

3:9

Paul evidences his winning the argument in having the Jews to gasp for one ray of hope as they ask: "Have we no defence, have we no protection, have we no shield?" And Paul cuts off all hope and plunges them into utter despair as he answers, "None." Then he states that no one, neither Jew nor Gentile, has any defence. To be "under sin" means that we are all sinners by nature, and thereby justly condemned as sinners before God. The term denotes the reign of sin, the reign of death, that is, sin governs to kill. πάντας (all) without the article denotes the individuality of the sinful state. Each individual is born in sin—no exception (Ps. 51:5; Eph. 2:3). The absence of the article further emphasizes the individual responsibility and personal guilt, as all are under the penalty and condemnation of sin; and denotes the universality of depravity, sin, guilt, and condemnation—every one guilty, each person condemned—individually, but universally, even to the totality of mankind.

It is said that Paul included himself among the universally condemned, in order that he might not give offence (cf. 3:8). But rather he included himself because he was born one among them, and was one with them by nature. He makes no exception—not even to himself; for he was the chief of sinners among them (1 Tim. 1:15). Therefore, he included himself among them, not to avoid giving offence but in order to deal according to truth, for he was born together with them under sin, with all its guilt and all its penalties, and with death as its condemnation. He included all under sin that all might have deliverance. All are shown under condemnation and death, that all might live through the redemption in the Slain Lamb. Man is rendered defenseless in order that unto God will be all the glory for redemption. God deprives them of every defense and shield in order that they, having no protection, will be free to take refuge in the covert under His wing, and dwell in His tabernacle forever (cf. Ps. 61:4).

3:10-18

Paul summons Scripture to prove the following:
1. The state of sin in character. 3:10-12.
2. The practice of sin in words. 3:13-14.
3. The practice of sin in deeds. 3:15-17.
4. The sinful source of the whole. 3:18.

3:10

"There exists not a righteous person," or, "there is none righteous, not even one." The δίκαιοι (righteous ones) are those who are just before God, those in perfect relation to Him. The unrighteous is ill-related to God; he is rebellious, unwilling, immoral, and at enmity with Him (See unrighteousness in 1:18). The absence of righteousness and the reign of immorality is the description of man universally. This is not Paul's, but God's description of man from Scripture (Ps. 14:1).

3:11

συνίων (understanding, from συν-ίημι). The verb means to understand. The participle is here used as a noun, and denotes a person having understanding. Paul gives a free negative quotation from the Septuagint of Ps. 14:2. "There does not exist an understanding one." The absence of the article denotes every one as destitute of moral and spiritual understanding. Sin has incapacitated them for making moral and spiritual discriminations. They can not distinguish the good from the evil. They do not know the line of demarcation between what is right and what is wrong. They are unable to make moral distinctions. God gave the description of universal mankind, when He said the people of Nineveh "can not discern between their right hand and their left hand" (Jonah 4:11). The totality of mankind is convicted of having no moral understanding—not a single exception, else God's all-seeing and ever searching eye from heaven could have found the exception.

Some so-called Christians are destitute of moral understanding. They give evidence of being unable to distinguish between good and evil, in that they cling to the evil saying, "I see no harm in it." No sense of guilt is the symptom of a dead conscience. A conscience made callous in sinful practice seeks to honor its deadness by such questions as: "Where is the line between good and evil?" "How can I distinguish between the two?" "Does it not depend upon the individual person as to how far one can go?" "Just how far can I go in sin and still be good or respectable?" "Just how close to the line of sin may I go?" "Where is the border?" The fool might just as reasonably ask how close he can come to the fire and not be burned. Though some may not come close enough to burn, yet they will have upon them the smell of fire—the fires of hell. Unregenerate human nature asks, "How little may I do?" The redeemed ask, "How much can I do?" The servant does as little as possible, while the son does as much as possible. No true husband would ask: "How may I give the minimum of love and fidelity to my wife, and how may I have the maximum of license?"

Love owes the maximum of duty and gives the maximum of service and permits no license whatsoever. The Christian can not serve the Lord and be all the time hunting for the borderline. Why does he want to find it, but to cross over? He can not be a child of the kingdom and live on the borderline. If the kingdom is in his heart, he will live in the heart of the kingdom, and not on the border. If he loves life, he will not want to march up to the borderline of death. If he is satisfied with the home land, he will not be seeking strange lands. Many have lived on the border so long that they talk like the children of sin. Many have lived so near the border that they look like the people on the other side. One can not love purity and enjoy bordering on the impure. He can not embody purity and live on the border of sin. There are a great many

professed Christians who do not exactly live in the world,
but they live so near the world that they do not bear any
fruit; they have not been exactly in the fire, but their
clothing has the smell of fire. They have no moral dis-
cernment. They can not make moral distinctions. They
can not discriminate between the good and the evil. They
"can not discern between their right hand and their left
hand."

ἐκζητῶν (seeking out). The "fool" in Ps. 14:1 is the one
without understanding, even the one in Ps. 14:2 from
whence this Scripture is quoted. The Hebrew word translated "fool" means "the withered one." His mind, heart,
and understanding are withered and twisted by indul-
gences in sin. His withered understanding can not discern.
His twisted mind can not discriminate. "The withered
one" has an affinity for the evil and therefore does not
want to discern the good. Thus, Paul adds, "There is none
seeking out God." God is looking down from heaven to
see if there can be found one that is seeking out God (Ps.
14:2). God's all-seeing, and all-piercing eye searches the
whole human race. He finds none righteous. The implication is not that God is hid nor has to be searched out, but
that man is lost and is not trying to find his way back
to God.

3:12

πάντες ἐξέκλιναν (all have turned aside). The absence of
the article denotes the totality, even to the last individual
as having turned from God's way (John 14:6) to his own
way (Isa. 53:6). They knew the right way. The Gentiles
knew it by the light of conscience and by nature (1:19f),
and the Jews by the written law (2:17-20) ; yet they forsake the way of God for the by-ways of sin.

ἠχρεώθησαν means unprofitable, worthless, useless, sour.
"There is none that doeth good." A good tree bears
good fruit. A corrupt tree bears corrupt fruit. Likewise, a
man's works are of the same moral quality as his nature.
What a man does grows out of what he is. Paul charged

that the totality of mankind was corrupt; and now he condemns the totality of their works as corrupt. There is none good, and there is none that doeth good. The singular is used several times in verses 11f to emphasize the totality—not even the exception of one.

3:13a

"Their throat is an open sepulchre." This is quoted from Ps. 5:9. The Hebrew word used for throat in Ps. 5:9 denotes primarily destruction. It first meant to gape, to yawn. Then the term was applied to a yawning abyss and gaping chasm. Then, from the idea of emptiness and empty space, the word took on a moral significance denoting appetite, lust, and passion. The predominant meaning of the word is destruction and death. But the term culminates in the words, speech, and language that is characterized by destructive chasms and deadly passions. These destructive words are as the yawning abyss, yearning to swallow to destruction and death every one who will listen to this deadly speech.

The throat denotes an organ of speech, but the emphasis is upon its primary function of swallowing. Thus, it denotes that the primary purpose of the speech is for destruction. The figure would resort to that of the ravenous beast, as its swallowing is the death of its prey. And the words of this throat are purposed to swallow up unto destruction and death all who will listen.

The nature and character of the words are described by an "open sepulchre." The open throat and corrupting discourse is referred to as the uncovered grave with the putrefying corpse lying at the bottom. Their words, like the unfilled grave, give forth an obnoxious odor of corruption and death. The form of speech here described is vulgarity. This vulgarity is not an occasional eruption of the grave. The "open grave" denotes the obnoxious vulgarity to be the continuous emanation of the destructive odor. The perfect participle being translated "open" denotes the vulgarity to be a permanent and hardened trait of character. The perfect participle indicates the permanency of the "open grave," that is, their vulgarity grows out of their corrupt nature; and their purposed destruction issues from their being dead in sin; and the repulsive and obnoxious odor coming from the decomposed corpse in the grave is a revelation of the rottenness of their own corrupt nature. The perfect participle further denotes the open grave to be the description of their nature rather than of their practice; it denotes depravity rather than occasional eruption; the emphasis is upon permanency rather than upon even frequency. Only the gospel of the faith-righteousness can close these open graves and silence the vulgarity of the wicked. Unless the gospel of Jesus Christ covers the unfilled graves, others will stumble in the dark and eke out a wretched destruction among the dead. Vulgarity is the essence of this expression, and is the most corrupt and obnoxious form of speech.

3:13b

"With their tongues they have used deceit," or their tongues make smooth, or slick, or oily. Hence, we use the expression "smooth talker" and "slick tongued." Their tongues are slick, smooth, gliding; that is, they speak flattery, deceit, and hypocrisy. Their tongues glide in flattery, in order to conceal the rottenness of their heart coming up through their throat, as the foul odor from a long dead corpse lying at the bottom of an unfilled grave. Here their speech is contrary to their nature. Their nature is as corrupt as a dead body that ought to have been covered long ago. Their speech appears sound, seems to have life in it, seems to be the only way to avoid destruction, professes to be the way of life, and a haven instead of a chasm. Their words entice, invite, and invent. The listener is disarmed by compliments, praise, and flattery. The corruption of heart is concealed in words of flattery. Rottenness lurks in pleasing phrases. The obnoxious odor is obscured by the fragrance of compliments. The unfilled grave is unseen at the feet of the slick tongued eulogist. The groans of death fade away amid the swelling euphony of words.

Hypocrisy is the epitome of the expression "With their tongues they have used deceit." It is flattery that they use, but they use it hypocritically. Flattery is their means; hypocrisy is the motive behind the method. Lying is included in the term. Hypocrisy refers to the whole realm of life as false. They used flattery to conceal the corruption in their hearts. Therefore, flattery gave a false profession of what lay concealed underneath. They sought to produce a fruit that would conceal the nature of the tree. The pleasant fruit is only to make you cling to the evil tree. The seemingly sweet water is only to make you drink deep and long of the water, whose bitterness shall make you bitter. The water is sweet only that it might be bitter. And the tongue is slick only that the innocent might slip and be found among the dead.

When olives are found on a fig tree, one knows they were just stuck on it. When true fruit is on the wrong tree, one knows it is not native to that tree; it is not there from growth—there is no life in it. With this combination of fruit and tree, the tree makes a false profession and the fruit is corrupt. Thus, some cursed lives bless a person at times. Yes, they bless him only temporarily that they might curse him permanently. Their goodness to him is to blind him to their curse. They are good to him only to obligate him to themselves, in order that he will follow when they lead him to a like cursed life. When they bless him they are most deceitful to him. When they bless him they curse him most. Their sweet morsel is only a bait to get him to swallow the whole of their bitter lives. They are vilest when they are best. They are bitterest when they are sweetest. They are basest when they are noblest. They are the most hypocritical when they come with flattery. They are most satanic when they ill garb themselves in the spirit of Christ.

3:13c

"The poison of asps is under their tongues" or "lips" (from Ps. 140:3). An asp is a most venomous serpent, the bite of which is fatal, unless the bitten part be immediately cut away. "The poison of asps" denotes that most poisonous form of speech used for the injecting of deadly corruption into others. The venom of slander is the pre-eminent and fearful idea in this Scripture. The most rapid movement of the adder's tongue gives the appearance of its being sharpened for the mortal wound. David knew that the serpent did not bite with its tongue, but this is the poetical and popular expression of its bite. It is thus spoken of because the tongue is so very closely associated with its delight and readiness to bite at the slightest disturbance and earliest opportunity, and because it is with the tongue that the slanderer does his like deadly work.

In the word "serpent" is the idea of being "coiled." "To coil" signifies both crookedness in life and the readiness to inject its poison at the slightest opportunity. Being coiled indicates the asp as inviting the opportunity to bite. Even when it crawls, it goes so crooked that it retains a part of its coil. This denotes the injecting of poison as the dominant element in the nature of the asp.

It is re-emphasized by this Scripture that the serpent has a seed in the human family. The slanderers are the seed of the old serpent, Satan, the devil. The poisonous venom of slander, slander without cause, and rapid working of the tongue give sufficient identification as to the children of the devil, and as to the seed of the serpent. They retain the venom of the old serpent, the devil, their father (John 8:44). They are, without disturbance and without occasion, shooting forth their poisonous slander. They would have others to think that the poison rightfully belongs to the one whose name they attach thereto, but not so. The poison is the inherent nature of the slanderer and is native to him. The poison belongs to the asp that does the biting. The venom belongs to the one doing the slandering. The one biting is the serpent. Therefore, when a person slanders another, crush the head of the serpent and not the one bitten; but seek to heal the bite and counteract the venom. Too often the listener crushes the victim, and lets the asp go free in a pure and healthy society. Sometimes an asp or two will get into a church, and some one or a group of people will begin to kill off the bitten ones, instead of crushing the heads of the serpents. The Good Shepherd would smite the wolf and gather His torn and bleeding sheep unto His bosom. The Father would crush the serpent and take His bitten children into His arms for healing.

3:14

"Whose mouth is full of cursing and bitterness." This is a free rendering of Ps. 10:7. "Cursing" denotes profanity; while "bitterness" denotes the hate, anger, and strife that always accompanies and follows in the wake of profane speech. The one cursing has fits of anger. The person of profane language is bitter and has bitter experiences with others. Fits of anger is the rule among those who curse. The profane person boils, hates, and embitters. The troubles of a person are multiplied if he uses profanity. There is little peace for the cursing one. Reverence in language is a person's best guarantee of harmony and peace among his fellows.

Vulgarity (3:13a) is the most obnoxious form of speech. Flattery (3:13b) is the most hypocritical form of speech. Slander is the most deadly form of speech (3:13c). And profanity (3:14) is the most inexcusable form of speech. There may be temptations for the first three; but there is never a temptation for a person to profane God's name. It is characteristic of man to sin by temptation; and it is characteristic of Satan to sin without temptation; therefore, to use profanity is to sin in similitude to the devil.

3:15

"Their feet are swift to shed blood" denotes crime with murder at the head of the list. Crime is the swift issue and result of the bitterness in verse 3:14. The first-born babe became a murderer. The second-born was murdered. The first family suffered from its victim and its criminal. The murder of Abel grew out of the great fury, rage, and wrath of the angry words of Cain (Gen. 4:5, 8). Murder is yet among the prevalent sins of the human family. Even nations have become murderers and have slaughtered by the wholesale method. Nations have been founded upon the ruins of others, and world powers have reached their strength by drinking the life blood of weaker nations.

3:16

"Destruction and misery are in their ways." "Destruction and misery" or "ruin and wretchedness" denote failure in life. Destruction is objective, while misery is subjective. The external denotes punishment and hardships; the internal denotes remorse, torturing of conscience and soul agony (cf. retribution and anguish in 2:9). Sin (murder, 3:15) caused the failure. Only sinners fail; and all sinners are failures. Failure is "in their ways"; but they have made their own ways. The plural of "way" denotes the multiplicity of human ways in contrast to "the Way" (John 14:6; cf. 3: 12a). The article with ὁδοῖς (ways, roads) denotes a definite way, that is, it reveals their determination in their ways—they are determined in their ways. "Ruin and wretchedness are in their determined ways." Their hearts are set upon their own ways.

3:17

"The way of peace they have not known." ὁδὸν (way, road) is singular, and is in sharp contrast to the plural of the same word in the preceding verse (cf. 3:16; 3:12a; John 14:6; Isa. 53:6). The "way" (singular) that leads to peace goes in the opposite direction to the "ways" (plural) which lead to "destruction and misery." ἔγνωσαν denotes experiential knowledge. They have never had an inner experience of peace. This verse denotes strife; but the emphasis is upon the inner strife of their soul and conscience as the source of all outward strife. They have no peace with others because they do not have within their souls the experiential knowledge of the peace of God. They do not know peace; they have no conception of harmony; they know only the strife that is raging within their nature. Criminals, murderers, sinners (3:15) fail (3:16) and never experience the way of peace (3:17). "There is no peace unto the wicked, saith the Lord" (Isa. 48:22).

3:18

φόβος θεοῦ (fear of God, godly fear, a godly reverence). The lack of reverence is the source of the several classes of sin as named in 3:10-17. Irreverence has been called the mother of evil. "The fear of (reverence for) the Lord is the beginning of wisdom" (Ps. 111:10).

3. *The above Old Testament quotations were made against the Jews in that they have the law.* 3:19-20

3:19

οἴδαμεν (we know) denotes a knowledge by eye-witness. Every observation proves that the whole of the Old Testament was written to the Jews. For fuller notes on this word, see the same word in 2:2.

ὁ νόμος (the law). The article denotes the whole law, that is, the law is a unity in its application to the Jews. The whole law speaks as one voice, and therefore addresses one people—the Jews.

ὅσα (whatsoever) does not denote "everything," but "anything." That is, whatsoever particular thing is said anywhere in the Jewish Scripture speaks directly to the Jews; and the whole law, being at unity, speaks through that one particular Scripture; and whatsoever it says is said by the unified law. Wherever the law speaks, it is by the authority of the whole law. Wherever a particular Scripture opens its mouth, the whole law speaks through it. A correct rendering of the thought would be, "Whatsoever is said is the whole law speaking," or "Whatsoever is said, the whole law speaks."

"We know from observation that anything the written law saith, it audibly speaketh to those in the realm of the law." λέγει (saith) refers to the contents of the law, while λαλεῖ (speaketh) refers to the outward, audible speech of the law. The first denotes the law as written; the second denotes the law becoming audible. The one denotes the record of the law; the second refers to the teaching of the law. We can see in the former, the reading of the law; and in the latter, the expounding of the law. In the one is the message of the law; in the other is the application of the law.

τοῖς ἐν τῷ νόμῳ (those under the law). The dative case denotes those in the realm of the law, those who live in the sphere of the law, those under the law by virtue of possessing it, and those to whom the law is addressed, that is, those who hear the law. The Jews had the law, they taught and heard it, and they lived with reference to it. It seems needless for Paul to remind the Jews that the law was to them; but he anticipated the above Old Testament quotations (3:10-17) to be resisted by some Jews on the ground that since the quotations were so descriptive of the Gentiles, they undoubtedly had no reference to the Jews. But Paul reminds the Jews of the unity of their law as it speaks to them. He condemns them by these Scriptures, in that the description pictures the Jews in Gentile vileness. It is thereby evident that the quotations are God's description of the Jews even from the time of David. These quotations show that there is no difference; and that all, both Jew and Gentile, as one vile race, are guilty and condemned under the judgment of God.

"In order that every mouth may be stopped." The Gentiles were condemned without the law; and the law condemns every Jew; therefore, no voice shall offer defense, no mouth shall contend for justification, no soul shall plead innocence, no life shall plead its righteousness, and their silence shall give assent to their guilt and condemnation. The fearful sentence from the awful judgment of God leaves the condemned in terror stricken silence. They are speechless because they are guilty, and because they can offer no defense; but the silence is chiefly from the terror excited by the vengeance of the invincible Judge of the dreadful tribunal of heaven and by the fear of the approaching abyss yawning to torment the souls with endless agony and unquenchable fire. Judgment and doom are always associated with guilt. Guilt and condemnation denote sin with all its issues in hell.

ὑπόδικος means under judgment, under sentence, under condemnation, one who has lost his suit, one who is condemned and only waiting execution.

ὁ κόσμος (the world). The article emphatically denotes the whole world, that is, the whole world of people—both Jew and Gentile. πᾶς (all, every one) gives added emphasis to the idea of universal condemnation. Interpret this word in the light of παντὶ (all, every one) in 1:16. The condemnation includes every one—both Jew and Gentile; but the emphasis is upon the Jews. The emphasis is not that the Gentiles are included, but that the Jews are not exempt from condemnation brought by their own law.

τῷ θεῷ (the God). The dative case denotes the realm in which the guilty are condemned. They are dealing with God. The article emphasizes the personality of God—the Personal God. This heightens the fearful nature of the awful judgment. (Read the fuller notes on the "judgment of God" in 2:2).

3:20

"By the works of the law shall no flesh be justified; for through the instrumentality of law cometh the knowledge of sin." This verse explains why the whole world is silenced under judgment. It is (1) because the law can

not save, and (2) because the law can only reveal sin
and bring judgment. The office of the law is not justification from sin, but conviction of sin and condemnation
for sin. The "work" referred to is the work of the law,
that is, the work that is required by the law, that which
is the fulfillment of law, and not mere works that might
be performed outside the realm of law.

δικαιωθήσεται (justified). This word means accounted
righteous, pronounced righteous, declared righteous, and
never to be nor to be made righteous. It denotes an
acquital, and may be said to include imputed righteousness but not personal righteousness.

σὰρξ (flesh) denotes unregenerate human nature in all
its corruption and depravity. The emphasis is upon its
susceptibility to sin. (For a further discussion of "flesh"
see "heart" in 2:29).

"Through the instrumentality of the law comes the
knowledge of sin" is the clearest and most concise statement that the Bible makes with reference to the office and
purpose of the law. A man will use a mirror to reveal the
dirt on his face, but he would be a fool to attempt to wash
his face in the mirror. The office of the law is not that of
salvation but of conviction and death—of prosecution and
execution. The law promises death, and never promised
life. The reverse is not in the power of the law. The law
kills but it can not make alive. It was given to convict
and not to convert; it proclaims guilt but has no cleansing
power. The law was given to condemn and not to justify.
Law must be just and never justify the guilty. It must
give justice and not mercy. The law convicts but can not
forgive. It prosecutes but never emancipates. Law offers
a penalty and not a reward. It reveals sin but can not
remove sin. The law lashes and leaves bleeding but it
can not heal the stripes.

ἐπίγνωσις (knowledge). γνῶσις (knowledge) denotes a
knowledge grounded in personal experience, experiential
knowledge, knowledge that is revealed through inner ex-

perience. ἐπὶ (upon) heightens the value of the knowledge. "Knowledge," with the prefix, denotes true, precise, and correct knowledge. Law gives a correct and experiential knowledge of sin. Sin is already experiential with the sinner, and law brings the guilt to consciousness.

ἁμαρτίας (sin, missing the mark, natural depravity, corruption in nature) does not denote sinful acts, but refers to sinful nature, the sin principle in man. The absence of the article, the word, the gender, the genitive case, the singular number, all support this position. The word corresponds to the Hebrew word חָטָא, to miss the mark, as when one throws or shoots at a target. It denotes the sinful disposition which leads men to miss the mark set by God, that is, the divine requirements. All the evil deeds of men grow out of this sin principle in man. Therefore, this word denotes the law as revealing, not only the sinful acts of man but also the innate sinful nature of man; not merely the sins of practice but also the sin in nature. The emphasis is not upon the acts of transgression but upon natural corruption. A person must repent, not only of his sinful deeds, but also of his sinful self; not only of what he has done but also of what he is (Isa. 55:7). God saves us from ourselves as well as from our sins. The sinner must forsake himself together with his sins (Matt. 16:24). The deepest conviction does not come from one's knowing that he had done wrong, but from his knowing that he is wrong. The emphasis of repentance is not upon turning from the evil deeds, but upon turning from the sin principle in nature which produces the sinful works. The convicted person knows that his guilt does not lie so much in what he has done as in what he is. The law convicts sin at its very root, and in its very nature; in order that grace may remove sin by its root and not by pruning its branches, and that grace may give a new nature rather than taming the old nature.

III

THE DOCTRINE OF JUSTIFICATION
3:21—5:21

I. JUSTIFICATION EXPLAINED
3:21-31

1. The nature of justification. 3:21-26.

> (1) It is without law. 3:21.
> (2) It is through faith. 3:22-23.
> (3) It is by the sacrifice of Jesus. 3:24-25.
> (4) This sacrifice justified God in the forgiveness of past, present, and future sins. 3:26.

2. The fruits of justification. 3:27-31.

> (1) It excludes the idea of merit. 3:27-28.
> (2) The unity of God proves the unity of the race and the unity of the means of salvation—faith. 3:29-30.
> (3) This grace establishes law. 3:31.

1. *The nature of justification.* 3:21-26

3:21

νυνὶ δὲ (but now) resumes for full discussion the thesis of the Epistle as stated in 1:17.

χωρὶς νόμου denotes without, apart, separate from law; it is equivalent to "no law." God's righteousness is a no-law-righteousness. The absence of the article from "law" denotes "any law," or "even one law"; that is, there is not even one law that can impart righteousness. Law has no part in salvation, no work in righteousness, and no offer of life. In this and in the next few verses, Paul shows that the righteousness of God is not contrary to law, though it is "without law." The law was never intended to save, and His righteousness is in perfect harmony to the law.

δικαιοσύνη θεοῦ (a righteousness of God, but more correctly, a divine righteousness). We are saved by substitution. We are saved by another's righteousness. Read the fuller discussion on this term in 1:17.

πεφανέρωται (hath been manifested). The perfect tense denotes past accomplishment with present and future benefits. The emphasis is upon the existing consummated state of the act. The middle voice denotes the "righteousness of God without law" to be self-evident—it ought not to need proving; that is, it is self-evident that law can not save; and it is self-evident that only God's righteousness can save; and therefore self-evident that law does not help God's righteousness to save.

"Being witnessed by the law and the prophets." This shows that the righteousness of God is not contrary to the law, but is the fulfillment of the testimony of both law and prophets. The articles with both "law" and "prophets" reveal the whole of law and the whole of prophecy to be at unity, in testifying with reference to salvation through the righteousness of God.

The genitive case shows the nature of law and the nature of prophecy to be in perfect harmony with God's righteousness. It further shows the testimony to His righteousness to be natural to law and prophecy. ὑπὸ (under) with the genitive case denotes a position under something higher. The subordination does not denote any imperfection in Scripture, but ὑπὸ (under) reveals the "law and the prophets" as only witnesses of the God Who saves. ὑπὸ (by, under) denotes the law and the prophets as voluntarily accepting, by their testimony, a subordinate place with reference to salvation and righteousness. The law reveals sin, the prophets revealed the sin-bearer, but it is God Who redeems. The law requires penalty, prophecy speaks of the sacrifice, but it is the Son of God Who is the Slain Lamb. The law demands justice, the prophecy promises mercy, but it is on the cross of Jesus where justice and mercy meet.

3:22

δέ (but, even) introduces a new division in Paul's subject of justification by grace, and denotes progress and development in his thesis. Having stated that we are saved by the righteousness of God, he now reveals faith as the method whereby the righteousness is appropriated to the individual. It is definitely stated here that saving faith must embrace Jesus, the trust must be in Christ, and the hope must be in His atonement. It is the faith in Jesus Christ that lays hold of salvation. Some who deny Jesus profess a faith in God. Such a faith is inadequate. Their denial of Jesus shows they do not believe God Who speaks in His Son (Heb. 1:2).

"The righteousness of God." (See same expression in 3:21 and 1:17).

Faith does not do the saving; but Jesus Christ, the sole object of faith, does the saving. The believer is not saved for his faith, but is saved through his faith. Faith has no saving merit; but faith can obtain Him Who has all merit.

εἰς πάντας (unto all). See this same word in 1:16 for a full discussion of it with reference to faith.

"For there is no difference" indicates again the common guilt of a condemned race. (See the discussion on 2:11).

3:23

πάντες γὰρ ἥμαρτον (for all sinned). The same analysis and the same discussion on "all who believe" in 1:16 can be restated here with reference to "all sinned." ἥμαρτον (sinned) refers especially to the sinful nature in man (cf. the same word in 3:20). The second aorist tense denotes the act as an historical fact, and refers especially to the Adamic sin.

There has been discussion at this verse such as "all sinned, but not all alike." There will be found a discussion of the difference and similitude of Jewish and Gentile sins in 2:1. But that interpretation can not be forced here. For this refers especially to the Adamic sin in every man. All sinned in Adam, and all sinned equally, and there is no difference in men with reference to the Adamic sin.

"All sinned, and fall short of the glory of God." The tense changes from the second aorist to the present. The present tense is used, because the Apostle thinks of the deficiency, as relating to the present state of the lost condition. ὑστεροῦνται (fall short), in the middle voice, refers the deficiency to their wilfulness, and charges the ones sinning for the deficiency. The present tense shows that they continued to fall short; they keep on falling short.

τῆς δόξης τοῦ θεοῦ (the glory of the God). If the article were absent from "God," then "God" would be translated "divine" and it would qualify "glory," and the expression would be translated "divine glory." But the article is present with both "glory" and "God"; therefore, it denotes the glory that belongs to the Personal God. Therefore, "glory" could not mean praise, honor, etc., as so many have imagined. That which man "falls short" of belongs to the Personal God, and does not emanate from man towards God. Man "falls short" of something that belongs to God now, and which man could now have. Man's falling short does not render God deficient, as would be the case if "glory" were interpreted praise, honor, etc. God has that in which man is deficient.

The root meaning of δόξα (glory) is value (See the discussion of the same word in 1:21). Then man "falls short of the value of the Personal God." The article is used with "value," as if to denote it as the pre-eminent value of God. The chief and fundamental attribute of God is His holiness. Then His righteousness is His chief value. Thus, the Scripture says, "all sinned, and fall short of the righteousness of the Personal God." This interpretation is in perfect harmony with Paul's thesis, as set out in this division of the Epistle. Also it is evident that Paul uses "the glory of God" synonymously with "the righteousness of God." He has been saying in this section that man has no righteousness, all mankind is without righteousness, there is manifested a righteousness of God, and because of inherent sin, man is deficient of God's glory. Thus, Paul is using "the glory of God" synonymously with "the righteousness of God." It is the righteousness of God that fallen man does not have; and it is the righteousness of God that man must have to be saved. Those sinning fall short of His righteousness; those believing are justified by His righteousness.

The first part of this verse denotes the character of mankind; the second part reveals the issues of sin. The first denotes spiritual death, the latter gives the reason. The one denotes the inherent sin, the other reveals the punishment. The former denotes the sinful act; the latter, its woeful consequences.

3:24

δωρεὰν (freely), that is, the righteousness is without cost to the believer; it is an unmerited gift; none deserve it, none can earn it, it is free, it is a gift—of mercy.

χάριτι (grace). See 1:5 for a full discussion of this word.

ἀπολυτρώσεως (redemption). This word explains how righteousness can be free to man. The word denotes a release by the payment of the ransom, a deliverance upon the ransom payment, and redemption at ransom cost. The word denotes acquittal, absolute and unconditional, upon the ransom payment. The believer is redeemed by Jesus Christ spilling His life blood for the ransom of many. We are redeemed at a tremendous cost, even the blood of Jesus, the Son of God. God had to bankrupt heaven to save a wretched sinner. The first part of this verse states redemption as a gift to the believer; but this word places the emphasis on the cost of man's salvation. It is free to man, but it cost God the highest price that was ever paid for anything. The soul of man is redeemed at such a tremendous cost that only God could pay the worth of one soul. It cost so much that even God could not pay the ransom price again. God set so high a value on the soul of man that He did not even spare His only begotten Son. The cross is God's estimate of the preciousness of a human soul. Anything that was corruptible, perishable, or human could not be a ransom price for redemption of a corrupt and perishing soul. In God's payment of the ransom, He valued the soul of man at the price of the blood, the agony, the death, and the life of the Son of God.

3:25

ἱλαστήριον (satisfying, covering, appeasing, expiating, propitiatory, mercy-seat). The root meaning of this word is to cover. This word is translated "mercy-seat" in Hebrews 9:5, and is the word used in the Septuagint to translate the Hebrew כַּפֹּרֶת , mercy-seat, that is, the lid or covering of the ark of the covenant. This word denotes the covering of the mercy-seat with the blood of the sacrifice on the day of atonement by the high priest. Though Meyer and others oppose this idea here, yet this is the most natural meaning to the word and to the text.

This word is an adjective and is more correctly rendered propitiatory rather than propitiation. Propitiation would denote the sacrifice, while propitiatory expresses the work of the sacrifice. Propitiatory carries the idea of priestly service as well as that of the sacrifice. Christ was both priest and sacrifice. The Gospels refer to Jesus as both priest and lamb; and the book of Hebrews speaks of Him as offering His own blood (Heb. 9:12), that is, He is both priest and sacrifice. This word denotes Jesus with His own blood, making expiation for the sins of those believing. Their sins being covered denotes the ransom as paid, accepted, and effectual.

Propitiatory is a New Testament word, while expiatory is an Old Testament term. "Propitiatory" means to satisfy, to cover. "Expiate" means to extinguish sins, to make sins not to be, to put sins out of existence. This is all that will satisfy God. The offering of the blood of Jesus upon the mercy-seat in heaven does this very thing. That

His blood does annihilate sin is supported by Scripture: "I have blotted out, as a thick cloud, thy transgressions, and as a cloud, thy sins; return unto me; for I have redeemed thee" (Isa. 44:22). "Thou has cast all my sins behind thy back" (Isa. 38:17). "As far as the east is from the west, so far hath He removed our transgressions from us" (Ps. 103:12). "Thou wilt cast all their sins into the depths of the sea" (Micah 7:19). "And their sins will I remember no more" (Heb. 8:12). "Behold the Lamb of God, that taketh away the sin of the world" (John 1:29).

ἐν τῷ αὐτοῦ αἵματι (in His blood). It is the blood that constitutes the sacrifice; it is the blood that is offered on the mercy-seat; it is the blood that perfects the atonement, and covers sins. The blood of Jesus Christ is the propitiatory sacrifice; and the efficacy of the blood is appropriated through faith in Jesus. The believer lives by substitution; and the life is in the blood. In Gen. 9:4, "life" is defined by "blood"; and in the next verse, "blood" is defined by "life." Lev. 17:11 says, "the life is in the blood," and Duet. 12:23 says, "the blood is the life." The two words used synonymously indicate inseparableness of the life and the blood. The believer lives through the shedding of the blood of Jesus. We do not live by His death, but by His life that He released to us in His blood. The emphasis of the atonement is not upon the death but upon the giving of the life.

The penal idea is in His suffering, the debt idea is in His death, and substitution is in both His death and His life; but the emphasis of substitution is in the giving of His life rather than in dying, since the blood contains the life. He died to pay our penalty, but He gave His life that we might live. The presenting of His blood on the mercy-seat in heaven was the offering of His life, and by faith His life is appropriated as His blood is applied. We are accepted on the basis of the blood; and in the blood we have our deliverance from the bondage of sin and death. The mercy-seat is on the level with the judgment-seat. We must go to God, not through the blood, but in the blood. His blood atones for our sins, covers our sins, and imparts life. Living in His blood, it is no longer our life, but His life that we are living, and our life is therefore eternal with His.

εἰς ἔνδειξιν τῆς δικαιοσύνης αὐτοῦ . . . (to show his righteousness because of the passing over of the sins done aforetime, in the forbearance of God). It is here stated that Jesus died to exhibit the righteousness of God. The cross of Jesus Christ is God's estimate of sin; and at the same time, it is a commentary on the righteousness of God. Jesus died to exhibit to the world that sin can not escape the punishment of God. And His death shows that in the last analysis that there is no such thing as forgiveness, but atonement and life by substitution. The cross remains a living monument to the fact that all sin will be punished—either in the sinner or in his substitute, and the life of the Substitute is appropriated through faith in His blood.

The cross is a revelation of sin; but more it is a revelation of the righteousness of God. It is at one and the same time the "revelation of His wrath" (1:18) and the "revelation of His righteousness" (1:17). Jesus died to propitiate man; but in a higher sense, He died to justify God in the propitiation. God had to guard His own righteousness or there would be no righteousness for the ungodly. To all those redeemed prior to the incarnation, the cross reveals to them the justice of God in punishing sins, in that their sins were punished and atoned for in Jesus, Who stood as a Slain Lamb from eternity. And the cross is a reminder to present and future generations that no sins shall escape punishment, and that none shall be saved except through the blood of the Son of God, Who gave Himself on Calvary as a sacrifice for the sin of the world.

The sins that were passed over, prior to the cross, were the forgiven sins of the redeemed. The sins of the doomed were not passed over, but are forever being punished in the transgressors. The sins of the redeemed were not historically punished till in the death of Christ on the cross.   God was not unrighteous in this delay of penalty. Their sins were not then dealt with in judgment, but were dealt with in His forbearance.   For a full discussion of forbearance see 2:4.

πάρεσιν (passing over) does not denote freedom from penalty, but a delayed punishment.   The redeemed are gone; therefore, their sins are never punished in them, but in another—even Jesus, our Substitute.   Thus, we see substitution in this word.   The word also means "dismissal"; that is, as far as the redeemed were concerned, their sins were then imputed to the Lamb of God, Who bore our sins from eternity.   The death of Christ is only the historical exhibiting of what has been in the mind of God from eternity.

3:26

The righteousness of God punished sin in the death of Christ, therefore God can forgive sin only in the believing sinner and be just to both the sin and the sinner. The righteousness of God is satisfied in the Substitute on the cross.   Then it is righteous for Him to save the ones for whom Jesus becomes the Substitute.   Jesus died that God might maintain His integrity in justifying the unjust. Jesus died for man, but more pre-eminently did He die for God (See "grace" in 1:5).

2. *The fruits of justification.*   3:27-31

3:27

Grace is a gift.   The very nature of salvation excludes any boasting.   The word translated "excluded" being in the aorist tense denotes "excluded once for all."

ἀλλὰ (but) is the strongest conjunction, and denotes the sharpest contrast between the "work method" and the "faith system"—the false and true way of salvation.

3:28

λογιζόμεθα (we reckon, we conclude, we are persuaded). This word denotes a conclusion drawn from evidence, that is, the evidence being all in, the conclusion is ready. In this word is the shout of a victor. The whole matter of justification by faith has been presented, and the conclusion from evidence is: "Man is justified by faith, apart from work of law."

ἄνθρωπον (man). This word carries the generic sense of humanity. It does not denote Jew nor Gentile, but is inclusive of all humanity. The singular number individualizes the multiplicity as one man, to emphasize faith as the one and only means of justification.

To be justified without works is to be without merit, not earning, not paying for salvation, not deserving life. It denotes one as being justified of God alone as a gift of mercy. "Grace" is the positive side of salvation, and "without works" is the negative side. The one is a statement of how God saves; the other states how God does not save. The one confesses God as the Redeemer; the other denies law as the redeemer. And both attributes salvation to the righteousness of God.

3:29-30

Paul has based justification on the righteousness of God; for fallen man has no righteousness, neither can he produce a righteousness, but must go to the source of life and righteousness. He based grace upon universal guilt; for from the very nature of their case, they can only be saved by grace since they have no merit. He based faith upon the unity of the race, as is seen in the notes on "man" in 3:28. And the unity of the race is based upon the unity of God; and thereby the universality of justification is based upon the unity of God.

The unity of God ensures His universality. If He were not the only God, He could not be universal. There can be but one God. Two Infinites could not co-exist. They would equal each the other, and therefore neither would be infinite. One Infinite fills the universe; therefore, another could not exist. Two Infinites would mutually exclude each the other. The unity of God assures the unity of the race. Genesis teaches that the entire race has descended from one pair. Paul tells the proud Athenians that God made one of every nation (Acts 17:26). The Scripture traces sin and death to Adam as the common father of all men. All nations came from God; and He is God of all. Christ was not the son of the Jews, but the Son of Man. He was not king of Jews only; He is the King of kings and Lord of lords (Rev. 19:16). Thus, the unity of the race is based upon the unity of God.

3:31

The law gave testimony of the righteousness of God through faith (3:21). Therefore, law and faith are in the same harmonious relationship, as promise is to fulfillment. The only way a man can be accredited with keeping the law is to appropriate to himself by faith Him, Who did keep the law and Who is the fulfillment of the law, both in obedience and penalties. The person who keeps the law is free from the law. The law does not fail but succeeds, when men are free from it. Men living above the law is the perfection of law.

The Old Testament Scripture is the Holy Scripture— the Word of God. Everything in it is true. Truth is eternal. The Old Testament is prophetic of the New. The New Testament is the heart of the Old—the revelation of the Old. Revelation does not abrogate the Old but establishes it. For example, when an artist finishes his picture, it does not destroy his vision, but it establishes, reveals, and proclaims his vision. When the architect finishes his building, it does not obliterate nor deny the blueprint. When an inventor perfects his automobile, he does not throw away his plans; those laws become operative in the perfection of the car. The Old Testament is the promise, while the New Testament is the fulfillment. The fulfillment does not deny nor do away with the promise. Neither has any law ever been done away with; for truth is not relative but absolute and eternal.

Christ did not do away with the sacrificial lamb; but He is the Lamb of God, Who stood as slain from before the foundation of the world. The ceremonies of the law were not done away with, but are fulfilled by Christian living. No moral law was ever canceled, but grace puts men under greater sense of guilt, and therefore heightens our conception of the meaning and requirements of every law. For example, the law said: "Thou shalt not kill." Jesus interpreted this law more fully than any lawyer or scribe before Him, as He pressed murder to its origin and source—hate; declaring hate to be criminal—and more—to be murder. Hate was embryonic murder in Moses' day, and hate is included in the Mosaic Law against murder. But the people limited the interpretation to violation by act, while Jesus presses it to its full meaning of criminal thinking, as well as the actual murder. Again, they interpreted their laws to require pure relationships, and Jesus said these laws include pure thinking in addition, and that the concealed flames of the heart render men guilty of adultery (Matt. 5:28). Jesus is not giving a new law, nor a revision of the old law, nor a heightened interpretation of the law, but He is giving a full interpretation of the law that had been limited in its interpretation. This interpretation was in the mind of God, though it might not have been in the understanding of man. Christ's interpretation has been the meaning of the law from eternity. And men are guilty and judged, not according to their frail interpretation of the Scripture, but according to God's eternal and immutable law.

We would be very poor if we had not the knowledge of the Old Testament, and we would be ignorant of the meaning of the New Testament. Without the Old Testament, we would not know where sin came in; and we would wonder what nations would be founded upon, had it not been

for the law of God. If we were to cast off what we obtained from the Old Testament, it would disrupt nations
and civilization in organization, in morals, and in every
other relationship. Therefore, the Old Testament Scripture must be of indispensable value to the individual
Christian and to organized Christianity. The Old Covenant shall ever go hand in hand with the New Testament
—the one as God's promise to man, the other as the fulfillment of His promise. The fulfillment of the promise
makes the promise more sacred; and the promise will
never be forgotten as long as we remember its fulfillment.
The promise can never be valueless as long as the fulfillment is valued.

II. ABRAHAM WAS JUSTIFIED BY FAITH

OR

THE PRIORITY OF THE GENTILES OVER THE JEWS

4:1-25

I. **The priority of the Gentiles over the Jews in grace** (if the Jew insists
on making distinctions); in that, Abraham was a Gentile before
he was a Jew, and therefore saved by grace and not by being
a Jew. 4:1-8.

1. The question opened. 4:1.
2. Flesh, works, and personal glory are at unity, but not with
   God and grace. 4:2.
3. Unity is found, on the other hand, in Scripture, faith, God,
   grace, and righteousness. 4:3.
4. Work, the things of the flesh, being a Jew, and debt are at
   unity, but not with grace and true reward. 4:4.
5. Unity is again found in grace, faith, justification, and righteousness. 4:5.
6. Also Inspired David, Scripture (Ps. 32:1f), experience, forgiveness, covering of sins, Jehovah (the God of salvation) are
   at unity in salvation by grace, apart from flesh, work, and
   law. 4:6-8.

Conclusion: Abraham was saved by Gentile faith and not by
the flesh of a Jew.

2. **The priority of the Gentiles over the Jews in faith** (if the Jew insists on making distinctions). 4:9-10.

   1. The question is raised as to when Abraham was justified by faith—in circumcision or in uncircumcision? 4:9.
   2. Scripture answers the question that Abraham had faith about twenty-five years before his circumcision. (cf. Gen. 15:6; 16:4; 17:25f) 4:10.

3. **The priority of the Gentiles over the Jews** (if the Jew insists on making distinctions) **from the standpoint of circumcision,** in that Abraham was circumcised to include the Jews and not to exclude the Gentiles. 4:11-12.

   1. The meaning of circumcision—a seal of righteousness by faith which he had before circumcision. 4:11.
      (1) He had righteousness as a Gentile—in uncircumcision. 4:11a.
      (2) He was saved a Gentile—in uncircumcision. 4:11b.
      (3) He was the father of the uncircumcised believer. 4:11c.
   2. The purpose of circumcision. 4:12.
      (1) To bring the circumcised Jew under the fatherhood of Abraham. The Jews were admitted to natural sonship upon secondary relationship to the uncircumcised Gentiles. 4:12a.
      (2) To include the Jew and not to exclude the Gentile. Circumcision would only prove the Gentile to be the natural sons of the uncircumcised, believing Abraham, and would prove the Jews to be adopted sons. 4:12b.

   Conclusion: Sonship unto Abraham depends upon grace and not upon circumcision.

4. **The priority of the Gentiles over the Jews from the standpoint of law** (if the Jew insists on making distinctions). 4:13-16.

   1. The promise was not through law, but through the righteousness of faith four hundred and thirty years before the law was given (Gal. 3:14-17) 4:13.
   2. Inheritance through law would make faith void and the promise of none effect. 4:14.
      (1) For law worketh wrath and death, and the promise is not given to those under wrath and the dead can not heir the promise. 4:15a.
      (2) No law would mean non-imputation of transgression. The Gentiles having the minimum of law brings their transgression to the minimum before God and in comparison with the Jew who has all the law and yet guilty of

breaking it all. And the rank heathen Gentiles without the law have a more direct claim to promise than the transgressing Jews do with the whole law broken. 4:15b.

3. The promise is by faith so the law breakers can be saved; thus, putting the transgressing Jew on equal footing with the Gentile. 4:16.

Conclusion: Sonship unto Abraham depends upon faith and not upon law.

5. **The priority of the Gentiles over the Jews from the viewpoint of the fatherhood of Abraham**   (if the Jew insists on making distinctions). 4:17-21.

1. Abraham was made the father of Gentile nations (and "nations" in the Greek means "Gentile nations"). 4:17a.
    (1) Thus, Gentiles would have pre-eminence in sonship.
    (2) Ishmael would have pre-eminence in natural sonship.
    (3) The natural sonship through Isaac, the child of promise through faith, would include and give pre-eminence to Esau over Jacob (cf. 9:9-13).

2. Abraham's children are spiritual sons (cf. 2:28). 4:17b-21.
    (1) Children of the resurrection. 4:17b.
    (2) Children of faith. 4:18.
    (3) Children of the supernatural power—children of God. 4:19.
    (4) Children of promise (cf. 9:8). 4:20f.

Conclusion: Sonship depends upon the spiritual nature of Abraham and not upon natural descent.

6. **The priority of Scripture over all authority for all time in matters of salvation.** 4:22-25.

1. Scripture is the authority as to Abraham's righteousness by faith. 4:22.

2. The Scripture is the final authority as to how all people are saved. 4: 23-25.
    (1) As to how Abraham was saved, but not to him alone. 4:23.
    (2) As to how all people of present and future generations are saved. 4:24a.
    (3) For Abraham and for all generations, saving faith is a resurrectional faith—faith in a resurrection. 4:24b.
    (4) The resurrection is the consummation and final word as to how men are saved. 4:25.

1. *The priority of the Gentiles over the Jews in Grace.* 4:1-8

The last verse of chapter three concluded that chapter, formed the transition, and introduced the theme of the present chapter. Paul proved in 3:21-31 that justification is apart and without the law. He gave brief mention of the harmony of law with justification by faith (3:21, 29ff). Now in this chapter, he goes at length to show the harmony of the law with justification by faith by citing the outstanding man of faith—Abraham, in whom the Jews largely find their grounds of boasting and hope. Paul takes the same man to prove justification by faith that the objector would take to prove life in the law.

4:1

The most natural rendering and interpretation is obtained by connecting "according to flesh" with "our forefather." The proper name, "Abraham" has no declension. In the expression "Abraham our father," "father" takes the case in which "Abraham" is used. This is true every time the expression occurs in the New Testament (cf. Luke 1:73; James 2:21).

’Αβραὰμ τὸν προπάτορα (Abraham, the forefather). The substantive is forced to take the same case with its appositive, which is the accusative. "Abraham" must be in the same case with "forefather" to be according to correct grammar. Thus, "Abraham" is in the accusative along with "forefather" and "flesh." The three words in the accusative reveal "forefather" and "flesh" to be the common appositives of "Abraham." Therefore, the verse should read: "What then shall we say concerning Abraham, our forefather in the flesh?" The three accusatives prove this rendering to be correct. Thus, the question is not, "What has Abraham, our forefather, found according to the flesh?" but correctly, "What then shall we say concerning our own blood-kin father, Abraham?" The Scripture does not inquire as to what Abraham obtained, but how did he obtain justification. "Hath found" is not present in the best manuscripts. Its presence would demand "Abraham, the forefather" to be in the nominative rather than in the accusative case.

4:2

Abraham had much to his credit—father of a nation, received a promise, and obtained justification. If he obtained these by work—by his own merit, he has likewise much in which to glory—in himself, but no occasion to glory towards God. The Lord deserves no glory for what a man did not get from Him. And a man may glory in what is his by desert or reward. It is indicated in the last of this verse that Abraham was not saved by works in that he does have a right to glory towards God.

4:3

Paul takes his readers to the Scripture to determine the method of Abraham's salvation. Genesis 15:6 records Abraham's faith as having been counted for righteousness.

ἐλογίσθη (reckoned, accounted, imputed) was used of old to mean "to set down" an account, and "to enter on record" transactions of business. The word was also used of recording the deeds of people, whether good or evil. The Bible often speaks of God's records in the Book (Ex. 32:32), the Book of Remembrance (Malachi 3:16), the Books (Rev. 20:12), and the Book of Life (Rev. 20:12; Phil. 4:3; Rev. 3:5; 13:8; 17:8; 20:15; 21:27). Abraham's name was entered on God's Book of Life because of his faith, that is, righteousness was credited to Abraham's account on the ground of faith.

4:4

"Now to him that worketh, the reward is not reckoned as of grace, but as of debt." Paul is here making a comparison from the everyday life of the laborer. Any time a man works, there is a debt that must be settled justly. The laborer is deserving of his merited reward. The wage is not a gift but desert. It would be an insult to the worker to call his hire a gift, mercy, free help, or grace. The laborer, by his work, has placed the employer under eternal obligation to pay the just reward. Likewise, God would be under obligation to reward eternal life to every one who earns it through work. But God is obligated to no man; and no person deserves life, nor do they have any merit whatsoever.

4:5

In this verse, Paul states the reverse of the preceding verse. He showed in verse three that Abraham was saved by grace through faith. Verse 4 proves that work excludes both faith and grace. This verse again takes up the theme and shows that faith, grace, and righteousness are related, and that they operate only in the absence of "work." As long as a person works for his salvation, he will not receive it. Faith can not be co-existent with the feeling of merit. The worker trusts in his work, in himself; while faith distrusts every earthly thing for salvation and clings to God and Him alone. God can not save a man till he quits trying to save himself. Nor can He save the one who feels deserving of life. Only those who know themselves to be lost and helpless will come for divine righteousness.

God is pleased to be known as "Him that justifieth the ungodly." This is God's highest title and His noblest work. It is not in the power of judges, courts, nor the law to justify the guilty. They must justify the just and condemn the unjust. God reverses this method by condemning those who profess innocence and by justifying those who profess their guilt in repentance and faith.

Many expositors have said that the designation of "ungodly" did not apply to Abraham. It applies to no believer as such, but it applies to every one in his unregenerate nature—including Abraham. Unregenerate human nature is sinful, corrupt, and ungodly. And the unregenerate nature of Abraham was no different from unregenerate human nature in any other lost person. The sin principle is just as sinful in the "moral" lost man as in the wretch. The transgressions do not degrade corrupt nature. Nor does reformation purify the corrupt nature. ἁμαρτία (sin in nature) does not get its sinful quality by the παράβασις (transgression). The sin principle is equally and utterly corrupt in every lost person, though they are unequal in transgression. The corrupt nature that transgresses less can only glory in the restraining power of the Holy Spirit, and of Christianity as it is lived by others. Except for these things, all sinful nature would be at its worst, and its worst would be only natural to the nature. He who is vilest is only acting in accordance with his nature. And the unregenerate nature that is milder is not better, but is only somewhat under subjection.

ἀσεβῆ (ungodly, irreverent) places the lost person at the greatest distance from God, and denotes the antithesis of God—the negation of God. The ungodly can lay least claim to merit and to justification. This word denotes the extent of God's grace and the power of His justification. (For a full discussion of "ungodly" see 1:18).

"Ungodly" denotes the subjects of His grace, and reveals how unworthy any one is of being justified. They deserve only condemnation, punishment, and death. But God justifies the unjust, bears in Himself the punishment of the guilty, and gives His own righteousness and life to those who only deserve death. He favors those who are under wrath, and forgives those who have sinned. Law can only defend the sinless. Grace can save only a sinner. Christ came to seek and to save the lost (Luke 19:10). The Physician came only to the sick (Matt. 9:12). The Shepherd goes out after the lost, and not to seek the ones safe in the fold (Luke 15). Only the unjust need justification (Luke 18:9-14). It is the ungodly that God makes godly. Through grace, the worst may become the best, the most wicked may become the most righteous, the vilest may become the purest.

4:6ff

We are sure of the Davidic authorship of Psalm 32, though the name of David was used as a synonymn for the Psalms. The whole of the Psalms, at this time, bore the name of David, though it was well known that he was not the sole author. David's words are not called as new evidence on justification, but as testimony of the way Abraham was saved. This Scripture is used to indicate the Biblical position on the subject of justification by faith. The quotation (Ps. 32:1) needs no explanation.

2. *The priority of the Gentiles over the Jews in faith.* 4:9-10

4:9

An important question is now raised as to when Abraham was justified by faith. If in circumcision, then he is the father of only the circumcised, and Paul's claim 'for the Gentiles fails. But if he was saved in uncircumcision, then the Jews have vainly hoped in being the children of Abraham in circumcision. This evidence from Scripture will be decisive for the claim of Paul or for the Jews. There will not be needed much more evidence, and one will have failed in the support of his proposition, and the other will have set out God's eternal plan of salvation. Perhaps the Jews feel a sure victory, and that Paul will surely get caught in his own net. The next verse answers the question, and convicts the opposition.

4:10

Genesis 15:6 records Abraham's justification. There is an unmeasured length of time between his salvation and the conception of Ishmael (Gen. 16:4). Most expositors leave the matter by saying that Abraham was a justified man about fourteen years before his circumcision. He was circumcised when Ishmael was thirteen years old, that is, Ishmael was in his fourteenth year (Gen. 17:25f). That would make Abraham's justification, God's promise of an heir to him, and the conception of Ishmael, all to be almost simultaneous. But undoubtedly, years passed between God's promise of a son and Abraham's union to Hagar. This period of time is about ten years, as Ishmael was conceived after Abraham had been in Canaan for ten years (Genesis 16:3). And Abraham's justification was very soon after entering into Canaan (cf. Gen. 13:3). The deliverance of Lot (Gen. 14) was about all that occurred between Abraham's entering into Canaan and his justification. Therefore, Ishmael was conceived about ten years after Abraham had been saved. Thus, Ishmael's birth marked about eleven years of grace for Abraham. Ishmael was thirteen years old, that is, he was in his fourteenth year when Abraham was circumcised (Gen. 17:25f). Thus, we see that about twenty-five years expired between Abraham's justification and his circumcision. However, the length of time does not enhance Paul's proof, as it is enough and sufficient to know that Abraham was justified in uncircumcision.

3. The priority of the Gentiles over the Jews from standpoint of circumcision.   4:11-12

4:11

Paul must explain the purpose and value of circumcision since it does not confer righteousness (cf. 3:2). This verse gives the relationship of circumcision and righteousness. Circumcision is the seal of righteousness through faith. It is the outward testimony of inward righteousness. It is the outward proof of inward reality. This is the visible declaration of the invisible work of grace.

The first part of this verse explained why Abraham was circumcised; now the latter part of the verse explains why he was circumcised after his justification. He was justified while in uncircumcision in order that he might also be the father of the uncircumcision. He was justified while in Gentile nature. He was saved a Gentile, and remained such long after his justification. He was the father of the uncircumcision long before those of circumcision were included. He was the father of the Gentiles before there were any Jews. If the Jewish argument would prove anything, it would exclude themselves rather than the Gentiles, as the Gentiles have precedence in priority over the Jews, both in Justification and in the fatherhood of Abraham.

πατέρα (father). The absence of the article denotes Abraham as the common father of the faithful. The article would have denoted him as the exclusive father of some one or some group.

πάντων (all, every one), without the article, denotes any one, each one, every one—but each individual one personally. For the full significance of this word see the same word in 1:7; and 1:16. In each reference, the reader will apply the exegesis of the word to the fatherhood of Abraham.

4:12

The preceding verse said Abraham was saved in uncircumcision, that he might be the father of all those believing, though they be in uncircumcision. The first part of this verse says that Abraham was circumcised that he might also be the father of the circumcision. This proves that he was father of the Gentiles first, and that the Jews were admitted to natural sonship in secondary relationship to the uncircumcised Gentiles. Thus, if the Jews would rest their case upon circumcision, it would only prove them to be adopted sons; and would prove the uncircumcised Gentiles to be the natural sons of the uncircumcised, believing Abraham. Nothing had to be done to include the Gentiles; and Abraham was not circumcised to exclude the Gentiles, but to admit the Jews. Thus, the Gentiles were sons of Abraham before the Jews were.

It is repeated that Abraham was not justified in circumcision, but was saved without respect to it. And the believing uncircumcision are his sons in priority to the circumcision. Thus, the fatherhood and the sonship of Abraham rest on faith alone. Either those of cirmcumcision or uncircumcision may be sons of Abraham through justifying faith—but neither without it.   Therefore, the case is won, proving that circumcision has no saving power.   Paul does not again introduce the subject, and only uses the word once more in 15:8.   He leaves the matter, having proved that, "It is not the Gentile who must come to the Jew's circumcision for salvation; it is the Jew who must come to a Gentile faith, such a faith as Abraham had long before he was circumcised" (Stifler on *Romans*, p. 75).

4. *The priority of the Gentiles over the Jews from the standpoint of law.*   4:13-16

4:13

Having excluded the idea of salvation by circumcision, Paul now makes a broad inclusive statement, which excludes all law as having any saving power.   The inheritance of the world was not promised through the instrumentality of the law "but through the righteousness of faith."   The promise was made to Abraham four hundred and thirty years before the law was given (Gal. 3:14-17).   The inheritance is obtained in Christ through faith, and not in Abraham by circumcision.   The gift of Canaan to Abraham and to his seed was a guarantee of the Messianic Kingdom, and of His universal reign when the continents shall be carved into the Kingdom of our Lord and His Christ.

4:14

The preceding verse said the promise was not made through the law; this verse says the promise could not have been made through the law; and the next verse tells why.

4:15

The promise is realized through faith, and both promise and faith would be annulled if the inheritance were only to those under law.   For promise and law are not synonymous but antonyms; and faith is the only provi-

sion for the obtaining of the promise. And those seeking
the inheritance through the law have neither a means nor
a promise. Law never gives a promise. Law never gives
anything. It can only mete out justice. It does not deal
in faith but in violations. It does not deal with the faithful but with the transgressors. It does not offer an inheritance but a penalty. It can not give hope but terror;
not a promise but death.

Paul argues that the promise can not be realized
through law, from the very nature of law. Promise is an
expression of love, while law is an expression of wrath.
The promise is a gift, while law is to pay the penalty of
sin. The prefix κατὰ (down), with "work" carries the
idea to work down, to exhaust. The law exhausts the
wrath of God. The promise is made through mercy, while
there is no place for either promise or mercy in the
agency of His wrath.

Paul says there is no transgression where there is no
law, that is, law and transgression are inseparably related. Paul here establishes the principle of a universal law
upon the principle of universal sin, and thereby excludes
from the promise every condemned sinner in order that
all might be heirs of the promise through faith.

"Where there is no law, neither is there transgression."
The absence of the article from "law" gives proof that
Paul was not speaking of the absence of the Mosaic Law
merely but of any unrevealed law, whether absent from
their hearts or from tablets. Where there is not a revealed law, there is no violation of law. The non-imputation
of transgression does not deny sin in nature. Where there
is no law, the transgression is not added to the sin in
nature. But where there is law, the transgression is
added to that of corrupt nature. Paul wisely selected the
term παράβασις (transgression, overstepping) instead of
ἁμαρτία (sinful nature). There exists the universal corruption of human nature, though violations be limited
among the heathen Gentiles. And Paul would remind his
readers that the heathen without the law are a law unto
themselves, and are guilty of transgressing the laws they

have. But their minimum of law brings their transgression to the minimum. Paul's chief purpose is to show to the Jews that the rank heathen Gentiles without the law have a more direct claim to the promise of God than the transgressing Jews do with the whole law. Paul sweeps away all Jewish hope in law and leaves them with only one ray of hope—Gentile faith. Then as they might have relied upon some other point of the law, Paul, by one sweeping statement, plunged them into deepest despair under the fearful wrath of the divine law. Then in this dense darkness, Paul holds out one ray of light to guide them in their aimless path. That one ray of hope is in their coming to Gentile position—faith.

Paul gave priority to the Gentiles over the Jews in the fatherhood of Abraham, in the faith-system of justification, in respect to uncircumcision, and in respect to the absence of transgression, that is, the absence of guilt. Each time Paul drove the Jews to Gentile position. In this verse he tells why—that the promise might be sure to all—by grace through faith. Then he makes a final statement to bring the Jews to Gentile position, as he identifies those of Gentile faith as "that which is of the faith of Abraham," and contrasts those of the faith of Abraham from "that which is of the law." Thereby placing Gentile faith in sharpest contrast from the Jewish hope in law, in order that all might come to grace through faith for the promise. And in summary of the verse, the faithful are the seed, the heirs, the redeemed, the safe ones, and the sons of Abraham.

Faith is the guarantee and the surety of the promise. It is by faith, in order that law might not annul the promise. If promise were in the realm of law, transgression would render the promise invalid. The inheritance is promised through faith, that it might be realized by transgressors. Grace being provided for transgressors, the inheritance can not be forfeited by transgression (cf. 5:20).

5. *The priority of the Gentiles over the Jews from the standpoint of the fatherhood of Abraham.* 4:17-21

4:17

πατέρα (father) being without the article denotes Abraham as the common father of all. The article would have designated him as a special father to a definite people (Note the same word in 4:12).

πολλῶν ἐθνῶν (many nations) being without the article denotes the number as unlimited in contrast from some favored nation. The number is limited only by the totality of believing nations. The absence of the article admits all nations, any nation, as the fulfillment of God's word, when He said to Abraham, "A father of many nations have I made thee" (Gen. 17:5).

ἐθνῶν (nations, foreign nations, Gentile nations). This word places the emphasis upon foreign Gentile nations in sharp contradistinction from the Jews. That is, God said, "A father of many Gentile nations, I have made thee." The emphasis is all in favor of the Gentiles' faith position. (See same word in Matt. 4:15).

"Making alive the dead" is the description of the character of Abraham's faith and of the power of the God in Whom he trusted. It was a resurrecting faith, a faith in the resurrection, in the resurrectional power of God, in the resurrecting God, and in the resurrection God. The immediate reference is to Isaac who was born out of dead parental powers. His birth was a resurrection. The more distant reference is to the dead sinner who is quickened into eternal life through faith. Then there is an ultimate reference to the bodily resurrection in the last day.

The faith of Abraham was based upon a resurrection. Abraham believed in all the divine attributes, but faith is the one characteristic—quickening faith of the dead—that wrought the quickening of his own dead powers. It is more correct to say that God resurrected life out of the dead powers rather than quickened the dead powers to produce life. The resurrection faith is the only type that will resurrect. Isaac, the child of promise, was a child of the resurrection. And the children of Abraham must be children of the resurrection. It is the children of the resurrection, who heir the promise. This excludes some modern people, both Jew and Gentile, who think it enough to believe merely in the existence of God.

God quickening the dead is not a strange act for Him. It ought not to startle man. Bringing life out of death, that is, out of nothing, is His natural way of working. His eternal method with man has been "to call the things that are not, as though they were." Out of nothing, He created the worlds. So it is not an incredible thing for Him to bring an infant Isaac out of death, and to quicken a dead sinner to eternal life and fellowship with Him. So the last part of this verse is added, that our faith might not be strained but strengthened, in that the quickening power of God is the eternal and natural means of His dealings. For all creation, both animate and inanimate, was created from nothing; and the future generations are as real to God as those already existing. It is no strain on God to deal with the non-existent as already existing. So the birth of Isaac is a true type of the spiritual birth of the believing sinners— born of God, born out of death—resurrected, and children of the resurrection. All of this is natural to God.

4:18

"Who in hope believed against hope." In a joyful expectant confidence, Abraham believed against what he knew to be humanly impossible. What he knew and what he was unable to do contributed against hope. But what God said and what God is able to do contributed to hope. He hoped in God against human hope. He hoped in God when there was no human hope. He hoped in God when there was nothing for which to hope. He trusted God without human evidence. It is folly to require human testimony when human powers have failed. He hoped, believing God equal to any occasion—even to do the impossible, "and being fully assured that what he had promised, he was able also to perform" (4:21). The believing hope is mentioned first, because it prevailed over, rather against (ἐπί), the other.

This Scripture clearly says that Abraham's faith hoped in God. Now, the same Scripture says equally as clearly that His faith opposed (ἐπί, against) any hope derived from his own powers. This faith is more than one that arose above human confidence; it distrusted human abilities. The harmony between faith and hope in God is measured and emphasized by the opposition existing between his faith and hope in nature. "No trust" is a weaker term than "distrust." The one is negative, the other is positive. The first is passive, the second is active. The one might be indifferent, the second would make a difference. The former has no relationship, the latter maintains a warlike relationship.

Saving faith, not only trusts God, but distrusts human nature. Man is never fully committed to God till he transfers all his confidence to Him—distrusting everything else. Distrust in human ability is to be more than negative; it is to be a vigorous, positive, progressive distrust. Abraham's faith revolted against his own abilities with the same vigorousness that it clung in hope to God. Saving faith reacts against human confidence with the same strength with which it turns to God. And faith takes hold of God only as the sinner releases faith in self. The lost person will not find faith in God's power to save till he looses all faith in his own inability to save.

"A father of many nations" is discussed in the exegesis of 4:17.

Abraham became the father of many nations as his faith hoped in God. So his children are those of faith and hope in God. And Abraham became the father of many nations by distrusting his own powers. Thus, his children are not those of natural descent. Faith became the new nature of Abraham; therefore, the children of faith, hope, promise, and those quickened from the dead are his natural children of his new nature. Therefore, the faithful are his natural children rather than those of natural descent. According to the flesh, the Jews are the great-great-infinitesimal-great grandsons of Abraham; but by faith, we are the sons of Abraham—belonging to the first generation.

6. *The priority of Scripture over all authority for all time in matters of Salvation.* 4:22-25

4:22

This verse says that faith was reckoned unto Abraham for righteousness. His faith was characterized by a resurrection. It is a resurrecting faith that saves. The faith must be in the resurrection Christ. Only the God of the resurrection can resurrect a dead sinner.

4:25

"Who was delivered up for our trespasses, and was raised for our justification." There are many correct viewpoints from which one can look at redemption. However, these many views can be summed up in two: the atonement and justification—the provision and its fruit. The generally accepted interpretation of this verse is that the resurrection was God's approval and acceptance of the atonement made by Jesus. But the resurrection of Jesus was more than an acceptance, more than a stamp of approval. Such a view would place all the saving power in His death and none in His resurrection. But the verse under discussion places the atonement with His death and attributes our justification to His resurrection —His life. We died with Jesus on the cross, but we live with Him in His resurrection. The believer lives through the shedding of the blood of Jesus. However, we do not live by His death, but by His life that He released in His blood. The emphasis of the atonement is not upon the death, but upon the giving of life; and the life was in the blood (Gen. 9:4). (See the fuller discussion on "the blood" in 3:25). In sacrificial dying, the emphasis is not upon the death, but upon the giving of life. The emphasis is not upon the spilling of the blood, but upon the releasing of the life which is contained in the blood; and herein is an intimation of the resurrection. The emphasis is not upon the penalty but upon the deliverance; not upon Abraham's dead powers but upon the living Isaac; not upon the dead sinner but upon the living and resurrected saint; not upon the dying but upon the resurrected Christ. Some worship the crucifix, and serve a dead Christ; but we worship a living Christ—the God of justification.

If redemption were only the paying of a penalty, releasing of responsibility, dismissing from suffering, and escape from punishment, then a dead sacrifice might suffice. But that sacrifice must not only pay the penalty of the wicked, but must be efficacious in making the wicked good. Jesus not only died to make the unjust just before a just God; but He gave His life that the ungodly might be righteous before a righteous Father. His death perfects the first, and His life consummates the latter. His resurrection is the consummation of His saving power. The penitent sinner dies with Christ, and the believer lives in His resurrection. The Christian not only dies to sin but lives unto Christ. The Christian life is not only a crucifixion but a resurrection. Baptism is a burial but its consummation is a resurrection. Christ's death becomes our death, and His life becomes our life. The cross breaks the power of sin, and the resurrection opens the power of God (1:4). Jesus died that He might give His life; and in our dying with Him, we are resurrected to live the life of Him "Who was delivered up for our trespasses, and was raised for our justification."

III.   JUSTIFICATION BY FAITH IS THE BELIEVER'S ASSURANCE OF FINAL SALVATION

5:1-11

1. We triumph in the hope of the glory of God. 5:1-2.

2. We triumph in the hope that is wrought out in tribulations. 5:3-4.

3. We triumph in the love of God, Who perfects our salvation through Christ. 5:5-11.

   1. Who died for us while we were corrupt and ungodly enemies. 5:5-8.

   2. Whose life is the assurance of the consummation of our final salvation. 5:9-11.

1. *We triumph in the hope of the glory of God.* 5:1-2

Paul digressed from his subject of justification by faith to prove that Abraham's justification was by faith. Now Paul returns to his subject where he left off at the close of the third chapter.   He gets back to his subject by the use of "justification" in 4:25.

5:1

δικαιωθέντες (being justified).   The aorist tense denotes the justification as being wrought once for all time. God's justification forever prevails, and never needs to be repeated.   The participle denotes the continuous progress that God's justifying grace is making from individual to individual. Thus, the word denotes that as grace is multiplied to a growing number of people, they also are justified, that is, saved once for all.

"Peace" is more than tranquillity of conscience; it is more than cessation of hostility.   Even to say it is the opposite of wrath falls far short of a correct definition. "Peace" must be understood as a positive blessedness. "Peace" is an inclusive term denoting the sum total of the blessedness and fruits of justification.   (For further notes on "peace" see 1:7).

ἔχωμεν (we have).   The present tense shows that we

have this blessedness now. Peace is the fruit of justification, and every justified person has this peace immediately.

πρὸς (with, to, motion towards) carries the idea of intimate and personal relationship as face to face, communion, and fellowship; and at the same time implies "motion towards." Peace has motion towards God, that is, there is affinity between peace and God. The preposition shows that there is ever a drawing relation between God and the person who has the peace of justification.

The articles with "God" and "Lord" emphasize personality.

Justification in the aorist tense emphasizes the assurance of salvation. Then is mentioned the peace that comes from salvation. And the verse is consummated in the word πρὸς (with, motion towards), which denotes fellowship with the Personal God and the Personal Lord. The Personal Lord is Jesus, the sacrificial Lamb, and Christ of the resurrection. Justification by faith produces assurance, peace, and fellowship; that is, it gives assurance of future life, fruits in this life, and fellowship with God and Jesus Christ both now and eternally. Justification is abiding, peace is immediate, and fellowship it eternal.

5:2

προσαγωγὴν (access) carries the idea of one being introduced into the private chamber of a monarch. Jesus is the introducer; the believer is the introduced; God is the King; and grace is the realm of the introduction.

ἐσχήκαμεν (we have had). The introduction is not a brief nor an occasional visit. The perfect tense denotes past accomplishment, present and permanent possession, and the deriving of eternal benefits. We have present and eternal access in this realm of grace. In this word is an intimation of the believer's privileges and of God's bounty; and of the believer's priesthood and of the heavenly Holy of Holies. This word denotes the resources of heaven as being at the disposal of the justified ones. The believer's free access to the riches of His grace is just as

permanent now as if he were already in heaven.   The
perfect tense places no limit upon the supply of grace,
and holds the present access to be permanent with eternity.   Grace is therefore the permanent realm in which
the believer lives. The security of the believer is founded
in the eternal grace of God, in which the believer has full
and permanent access through Jesus Christ. Omnipotence
can not make assurance any more sure; and inspiration
can not reveal assurance in any stronger terms.

"We have had access" denotes more than a permanent
audience with the King; it denotes priestly entrance into
the Holy of Holies.   In this expression we see the universal priesthood of believers with an eternal approach to
the throne of grace, in contradistinction to the annual
entrance of the Jewish highpriest into the Holy of Holies
(Heb. 10:19-25). The believer may come boldly to the
throne of grace without the mediation of any human
(Heb. 6:17-20; 10:19).   When Jesus died on the cross,
the veil of the temple was rent in twain from top to
bottom (Matt. 27:51)—opening the Holy of Holies to
every believer as a priest unto himself.

ἐστήκαμεν (we stand).   Here again inspiration gives us
the force of the perfect tense.   As stated above, the perfect tense denotes past accomplishment, present and
permanent possession, and the deriving of eternal benefits.   This word, in the perfect tense, means we have had
standing, we have had immovable and unshakable establishment, we permanently stand in eternal safety.   We
have immovable and permanent establishment in the
grace into which Jesus led us for eternal access.   "We
have permanent access" and "we have permanent standing" in the eternal grace of God.   Words for assurance
are exhausted, and inspiration gives increased assurance
only by multiplying the perfect tense.   God deposited His
gospel in the strongest and most perfect language, in
order that we might have every assurance.   God wants
us to know; for where there is the lack of assurance there
is also the lack of faith.   Doubt is unbelief—the enemy

and the opposite of faith. Assurance is native to the character of our salvation; it is the ground for Christian joy, and it is the essence of our hope in God.

καυχώμεθα (we glory, we rejoice) denotes a shout of triumph. We are victoriously saved, and we give a shout of triumph in our hope of the glory of God. We shout because we have triumphed for eternity in assurance, in peace, in fellowship, in access to the throne of grace, in immovable establishment in grace, triumph in hope, and in the glory of God. The present triumph in these, together with the absolute assurance of their being consummated in heaven, is enough to produce rejoicing, glorying, and shouting. The shouts of triumph belong only to those who have the assurance of the glory of God.

ἐλπίδι (hope) is not to be understood in the degenerate sense that some use it. It does not mean to wish nor to blindly expect. "Hope" is the perseverance of faith. It denotes the assurance of salvation together with the joyful, peaceful, and restful confidence in which one waits for the consummation of his assurance. Only those who have the assurance of salvation have the hope of the glory of God. A person can have salvation without having the assurance, but he misses the joy of the hope. The idea of the security of the believer is exhausted in the word "hope."

τῆς δόξης τοῦ θεοῦ (the glory of the Personal God). Study the exegesis of "the glory" in 1:21, and especially the exegesis of "the glory of the God" in 3:23. And hold in mind that the believer has present possession of "the glory of the God" though it is consummated in heaven.

2. *We triumph in the hope that is wrought out in*

tribulations. 5:3-4

Paul has shown that justification by faith will stand the test of the future. Now he shows it will triumph over the present, however great the tribulations may be.

"We rejoice in our tribulations," that is, we give a shout of triumph even in tribulations. "Tribulations" are the external hardships that give hindrance in this life (See the notes on 2:9). Tribulations produce patience, steadfastness, and endurance, as the wind makes the young tree to root deeper and more firmly. Tribulations harden the runner for the race and give the believer endurance. The metal is purified by fire; so character is seasoned in trials. The endurance or steadfastness gives worth, and produces character that has stood the test. It denotes strength that has proven itself, and therefore is approved. And approvedness gives hope. Therein is the consciousness of a proven test. Tribulation does not weaken, but strengthens hope. Tribulation does not defeat the believer, but gives an occasion for triumphing in hope. We give a shout of triumph over tribulations as hope leads on towards heaven. Assurance transcends trouble; and the assurance of eternity transcends the storms of time.

3. We triumph in the love of God, Who perfects our salvation through Christ.   5:5-11

5:5

Beginning with this verse through verse 11, Paul shows a third time how hope will triumph. In 5:2, Paul said our hope will triumph because it is founded in the eternal grace of God. In 5:4, he gave tribulation as a second reason for the triumph of hope. In our present verse, he says hope will triumph because it rests in the abundant love of God, which gives full assurance of final salvation.

Hope can not disappoint. The assurance of salvation will never shame the believer. Hope will never embarrass. The reason hope never puts to shame is because God gives what He promises. Assurance is real, hope is in God, and God is true. Hope rests in the love of God, His love is poured upon us in abundance, and His love was exhibited to us in the death of Christ while we were wicked sinners.

"The love of God" is the ground of our hope. Our assurance is heightened by His generous love to us. He does not send His love as dew drops, nor in light showers as the rain, but like a flood does His love pour in upon the thirsty believer. "Heart" is mentioned as the recipient of His love, since the heart is the center of man's moral nature (See "heart" in 1:21). God's love went to the center of man's corruption to purify, to redeem, and to give assurance of a glorified life. The Holy Spirit was the agent, that followed the sinner and made known the love of God and the sacrifice for sinful man.

5:6

This verse points to the death of Christ for sinners as the proof of God's love for the believer. Christ died for us, not while we were clothed in the righteousness of God but while we were objects of divine wrath. The "weak ones" signifies the disease-ridden that have no hope of life. The term, morally used, denotes spiritual impotence from willful indulgence in sin, those that are purposely weak, and therefore powerless for good.

ὑπέρ (for, above) denotes substitution (See the exegesis of this word in 8:31).

"The weak ones" are here identified with the "ungodly," and are later called sinners (5:8) and enemies (5:10). While we were yet weak, we were "ungodly"— weak for good but strong for sin. The ungodly were helpless and powerless to produce good works. They were under wrath and deserved no mercy. They were unlovely, hateful, and hating. Yet God flooded His love upon the ungodly, and exhibited His love for them in the death of Christ. This is the most unlikely bestowal of love, and therefore the greatest reach of love. To die for another is the greatest expression of love; and to die for the ungodly is to love beyond comprehension (See notes on "ungodliness" in 1:18).

5:7

δικαίου (a just one, a righteous man) denotes the law-abiding person. He lives lawfully, and is just in the eyes of the court and law. External morality is emphasized in this designation.

τοῦ ἀγαθοῦ (the good man) denotes moral quality in addition to conformity to law. A man may be subject to every law with a rebellious spirit (See "in the spirit" in 2:29). "The good man" embodies the virtues expressed in the law.

It would be indeed difficult to find a person, who would be a substitute in death for a man whose righteousness has barely escaped penalties, and whose character terminated at the extremity of the reach and power of law. The absence of the article from δικαίου (a just man) denotes individuality, any just man, any law-abiding individual. The absence of the article limits the number to "possibly one." That is, there is scarcely one among all just men for whom there could be found a substitute in death. "Hardly, or scarcely," "just one," absence of the article, and "die" practically signify the impossibility of a substitute for "a just man."

There is more possibility, yet very little, that some one might venture to die for "the good man." The presence of the article with ἀγαθοῦ (good one, or good man) designates personality, a person who is good; and denotes the person as altogether possible, though very little hope of finding a person who will dare to die even for him. It would be extremely difficult to find a person who would die for a "just man"; it would be a rare case to find a substitute for even "the good man"; and it is beyond any human to die for the "ungodly."

5:8

A love that is beyond anything human is exhibited in Christ's dying for corrupt humanity. Those for whom Christ died, and whom God loves are both ungodly in practice and corrupt in nature. ἁμαρτωλῶν (sinners) denotes corrupt nature rather than transgression, and is the source of transgression. (See "sin," corrupt nature, in 3:20). For notes on "commendeth," see 3:5.

5:9

δικαιωθέντες (being justified). See the notes on this word in 5:1.

ἐν τῷ αἵματι (in the blood). See the notes on this expression in 3:25.

Since the death of Christ saved us, much more will His life keep us saved. Since His death evoked faith in us, much more does His life give us assurance. Since we triumphed over sin through His death, much more do we triumph in life through His life. Having loved us to die for us, much more can He exhibit His love in that He lives for us. Since His death perfected our life, much more will His life preserve our life. His life perfects even more than His death. His life is the most powerful virtue of His redemption. (See the notes on 4:25).

5:10

Since the death of Christ reconciled vicious enemies to God, much more is His life powerful for keeping saved those who are God's loved ones through reconciliation. Christ's death, changing the nature of enemies, gives absolute assurance that His life will preserve the godly nature of the children. Since God gave His only begotten Son in death to transform corrupt enemies into children, much more will the undying Trinity be dedicated to the children of the same life and nature. The death of Christ wrought life in the lost when there was no hope. Therefore, it would be wicked to gather no assurance from His life. The hope that came through death is magnified in His life.

God loves the ungodly (5:6), He justifies the sinner (5:8), and reconciles the enemies (5:10). His love accomplishes its work through the death of Christ. Much more does He love the good, and preserve the life of the righteous, and give final salvation to the reconciled. Hope

is born out of death and consummated in life. Miserable
is he who trusts less to the life of Christ than His death
initiated. And blessed is the man who has blessed assurance.

"Blessed assurance, Jesus is mine!
O, what a foretaste of glory divine!
Heir of salvation, purchase of God,
Born of His Spirit, washed in his blood."

5:11

καυχώμενοι (we glory, we rejoice, we give a shout of
triumph) is here used for the third time in 5:1-11. "We
give a shout of triumph in the hope of the glory of God"
(5:2) ; "and not only so, but also, we give a shout of triumph" in the hope that is wrought out in tribulations
(5:3) ; "and not only so, but also, we give a shout of triumph" in the love of God, Who perfects our salvation
through Him, Who died for us while we were corrupt and
ungodly enemies, and Whose life is the assurance of the
consummation of our final salvation (5:5-11). Assurance
of eternal life triumphs in grace, triumphs even in tribulations, and triumphs in the love of God towards us,
which is exhibited in Him, Who died to save us and Who
lives to keep us saved.

Grace perfects our salvation and gives assurance
(5:1f) ; tribulations of this life can not defeat our justification in grace, but only tends to increase our assurance
and hope (5:3f) ; and the love that died for us will live
for us unto the consummation of our assurance and hope
(5:5-11). Redemption triumphs and gives assurance at
the time of conversion (5:1f), during the perils of life
(5:3f), and in eternity (5:5-11). This passage of Scripture (5:1-11) exhausts the fundamental ideas of assurance, hope, and security for the believer.

IV. THE GRACE OF CHRIST TRANSCENDS THE
OFFENSE OF ADAM

5:12-21

1. Universal reign of sin came through one offense. 5:12.

2. Death comes from sinful nature rather than from transgression. 5:13-14.

3. The grace of One abounds unto many. 5:15.

4. The grace of Christ contrasted from the sin of Adam. 5:16-17.
   1. Condemnation came in Adam, but justification comes to as many as believe. 5:16.
   2. Death reigned in all through one; much more will grace reign in life through one, even Jesus. 5:17.

5. The grace of Christ compared with the sin of Adam. 5:18-21.
   1. All died in Adam, and all may be saved in Christ. 5:18.
   2. As the offense of Adam made men sinners, so the atonement of Jesus makes them righteous. 5:19.
   3. Where sin abounded, grace did much more abound. 5:20.
   4. As the relation to Adam brings certain death, so faith in Christ gives assurance of eternal life. 5:21.

1. Universal reign of sin came through one offense. 5:12

5:12

The word translated "sin" throughout this section denotes corrupt and fallen nature, as the direct issue of the original sin of Adam (See "sin" in 3:20).

ὁ θάνατος (the death) denotes both physical and spiritual death, with the emphasis on spiritual death. The article could refer to nothing short of spiritual death.

πάντες ἥμαρτον (all sinned). Both the word and the aorist tense denote this sin to be Adamic. The aorist tense denotes that "all sinned once for all time." When Adam sinned, all sinned in that all were in Adam. All sinned as one individual and as a race, for all the race was present in Adam. However, to say that all sinned collectively in one man is to lay emphasis and guilt upon Adam rather than holding each individual personally guilty for the Adamic sin. We did sin collectively in Adam; and more we sinned individually and personally in Adam. The absence of the article here renders the expression: "Each individually sinned once for all time." This denotes the permanent effect of that first sin. It further denotes individual responsibility and guilt in the Adamic sin. No sinner can blame his sinful nature to Adam alone. The fallen must accept the sin and guilt as individual, for he was present and had a part in the sin of Adam. And every descendant of Adam is just as guilty as was Adam; and he is personally guilty with Adam. Sin brings death; therefore, the totality of mankind died when the totality sinned in Adam. Universal sin brought universal death. All sinned in Adam, and all died in Adam. All were responsible in the sin, and all are guilty in the death.

2. *Death comes from sinful nature rather than from transgression.* 5:13

5:13

We still have the term ἁμαρτία (sin) which refers to the corrupt human nature, the sin-principle, and the depravity of fallen man. Corrupt and fallen human nature was innate with all before the giving of the Mosaic Law. The sin-principle antedates the law. Death reigned before Moses as well as afterwards.

4:15 is clear that there is no transgression, that is, violation of law, where there is no law. But the word used here is not παράβασις (transgression), but ἁμαρτία, which denotes the sin-principle, natural corruption, and innate sinful nature. This corrupt nature would not have been imputed except in violation of law. Yet it is imputed in the absence of the Mosaic Law. Therefore, it must be in violation of another law. Natural corruption and death came in Adam's violation of God's first commandment which said: "But of the tree of the knowledge of good and evil, thou shalt not eat of it: for in the day that thou eatest thereof thou shalt surely die" (Gen. 2:17). The sin-principle is not imputed from the sin of Mother Eve who violated no direct law—having heard none from God. We fell and died in Adam, whose sin violated the direct command of God. Sin is not reckoned where there is no law, but where it is imputed there is implied a law. Sin was imputed before the law of Moses; therefore, it was in violation of a previous law—the direct command of God to Adam in the garden. Therefore, death came not by the law of Moses, but reigned before Moses in the violation of God's first law and direct commandment. Neither does death come from transgression, but from inherent sinful nature.

5:14

Death reigned as a monarch before Moses, in that all had violated an earlier law. "Even over them that had not sinned after the likeness of Adam's transgression" denotes them as not sinning against revealed law. Adam violated a known law; these died without violating a revealed law; none die except by violation of law; therefore, they died for Adam's violation. There παράβασις (transgression) differs from that of Adam's in that Adam violated a known commandment that carried the penalty of death; but their ἁμαρτία (sin, corrupt nature) is identical with that of Adam, being brought by Adam. It was not the sin of practice that brought death to men from Adam to Moses; but death came from the sin of nature. They were sinners by nature before they were sinners by practice. They died without transgression being imputed by the Mosaic Law. They died because the principle of death came upon all in the Adamic sin. Their sin and death came in the sin of Adam and not from the Law of Moses. And men died from inherent sin before they had personal transgressions from the Mosaic Law. Men die from natural corruption and inherent sin even though they have no law to impute personal transgression.

3. *The Grace of One abounds unto many.* 5:15

5:15

"But not as the trespass, so also is the free gift" denotes that the sin of Adam and the righteousness of Christ are to be contrasted. The parallel of the two has not been drawn in the previous verses, but inferred.

By the sin of one man, death reigned over many. But the grace of God as a gift likewise abounds unto many. Death came from sin by natural issue, while the grace of God proceeds from Him as a gift. Inherent sin rendered men helpless in that they died of themselves; but "gift" and "grace" refer the whole responsibility of salvation to the resources of God; that is, death resides in man, while salvation resides in God; and sin is inherent in man, while life is inherent in God. But the grace of Christ is mightier than the depravity from Adam; and the grace of God plus the grace of Christ are mightier than the sin of one creature. God is wonderfully able to undo and re-create all that the sin of Adam wrecked.

4. *The Grace of Christ Contrasted from the Sin of Adam.*

5:16-17

5:16

The grace of Jesus is contrasted from the sin of Adam. Grace perfects in all believers what sin wrecked in one, Adam. Sin entered by one man from one offense. Grace was given according to the accumulated sins of the multiplied transgressions. Death came by one offense; grace covers multiplied offenses. And what sin did in Adam, God re-creates in countless millions. The offense of one met with the justice of God; while the offenses of the many were met with the mercy of God in the forgiveness of sin through the sacrifice of Jesus. The one offense appealed only to the judgment of God; while the many offenses appeal through the blood of Jesus unto the justification of every one believing. The one sin stirred God's wrath; the many sins stir Him to compassion, loving-kindness, mercy, and grace. The one sin of Adam occasioned his sentence of condemnation; while myriads of sins drew the mercy of God unto the justification of millions. The ratio of the redeemed of Adam determines the ratio of the relative power of grace over sin; of life over death, and of Christ's atonement over Adam's offense.

5:17

This verse is founded somewhat upon the superiority of grace as revealed by the contrast in the preceding verse. The unity of Adam's offense and multiplicity of Christ's work of grace are now considered with reference to the reign of death and the reign of life respectively. Read again the exegesis of 5:16, and apply the superiority of the justification of many over the condemnation of one, and you will have the magnitude of the reign of life in the millions over the reign of death through one. Since death reigns through one, much more will life reign through Christ since His seed have the abundance of grace and the gift of the righteousness of God. Trespass, Adam, and death are contrasted from grace, gift, righteousness, life, and Jesus Christ. The latter list is able to perfect more than the first series destroyed. The believers cease to live as rightful subjects under the domain of death, and are born children in the domain and under the reign of the Eternal King who was the Slain Lamb.

5. *The grace of Christ compared with the sin of Adam.* 5:18-21

5:18

The one righteous act of Jesus, perfects more than the one sinful act of man destroyed. The superiority of the one over the other is measured by the magnitude of justification over condemnation.

5:19

Likewise, the disobedience of one man, with its consequences of many sinners, is superseded by the obedience
of One, with its resulting consequence of many being
made righteous.

5:20

Man died from inherent sin before the law of Moses.
The law came to bring added guilt through transgression,
and to reveal the penalty of sin. The law revealed the
sinfulness of sin, and placed sin in its proper light. The
law heightened the guilt of the sinner, and revealed the
true nature of sin, and stirred sin to abound in trespasses.
But where sin abounded, grace did much more abound.
Where there was guilt, there was more grace. Where
there was sin, forgiveness was multiplied. When sin is
most powerful, then grace is most mighty in deliverance.

5:21

Death reigned through one (5:7) unto all (5:14, 12).
This monarch reigned by reason of the rightful subjects
of his domain. Sin is also a reigning king. This monarch
of sin reigns in the dominion of death. His subjects are
governed to one end and purpose—death. This monarch
is an enemy to his subjects, yet they love, obey, and serve
him with delight. Grace is also a personified king. His
subjects are the redeemed, his dominion is righteousness,
and his government is unto life eternal, through Jesus
Christ our Lord.

IV

THE DOCTRINE OF SANCTIFICATION
6:1—8:39

I. THE BELIEVER'S RELATIONSHIP TO SIN
6:1—7:6

1. Dead to the principle of sin. 6:1-14.
   1. Grace gives no license. 6:1.
   2. The dead cease from former activity. 6:2.
   3. The burial in baptism denotes Christians as dead to sin. 6:3-4a.
   4. Rising from baptism pictures the resurrected life in Christ. 6:4b-5.
   5. The death to sin is once, and the life unto God is eternal. 6:6-11.
   6. Sin must not reign over the members of those who are dead to sin. 6:12-14.

2. Dead to the practice of sin. 6:15-23.
   1. Grace does not encourage lawlessness. 6:15.
   2. Ye are the servants of whom ye serve. 6:16.
   3. Ye are the servants of righteousness. 6:17-18.
   4. Serve righteousness as faithfully as you did sin. 6:19.
   5. The fruit of the Christian does not shame. 6:20-22.
   6. Sin pays death for service; but God gives eternal life to the believer. 6:23.

3. Dead to the power of sin. 7:1-6. (cf. I Cor. 15:56).
   1. The law is well known to the Jews. 7:1.
   2. Law is binding only in life as is the case of the marriage vow. 7:2-3.
   3. Those who die to sin are dead to the law, and are free to be joined to Christ. 7:4.
   4. The former relationship with sin demanded service, but it was unto death. 7:5.
   5. The new relationship with Christ, likewise, produces a new devotion—to "serve in the newness of the spirit." 7:6.

161

1.The believer is dead to the principle of sin. 6:1-14

In 3:21—5:21, Paul proved his thesis of Justification by Faith. This justification by faith obtained the imputed righteousness of God, but did not give personal righteousness. Through chapters 6-8, Paul discusses sanctification, to prove that justification by faith produces moral character in addition to obtaining the imputed righteousness of God. That is, God justifies the sinner and then makes the believer like Himself—righteous. Justification saves us; sanctification develops us. Justification delivers from the penalty of sin; sanctification delivers from the power of sin. The first declares us righteous, the second makes us righteous. The one is instantaneous and final, the other is gradual and sure. The former bears us, the latter grows us. The one is our nature, the other is our nurture. The one is imputed, the other is engendered. Both are of God and from God; neither is personal to the believer, but both are the work of grace and come through faith to make the person in character, nature, and righteousness of God.

Paul has set out and proved that the believer is saved by grace through faith in the blood of Jesus (3:24f) without the works of the law (3:20, 21, 28). The remainder of the Bible, in its entirety, corroborates with our experience in supporting Paul's thesis as the Gospel of God for salvation. Yet a vast host of Bible readers ignore God's revelation of scriptural righteousness, and follow the Pharisaic justification by law and the self-obtained righteousness in the covering with leaves. All those who believe in salvation by works, wholly or partially, transfer the redemptive power from justification to sanctification. We are born anew in justification and not in sanctification. Sanctification is not the ground of our salvation, but the fruit of justification. Sanctification, as the work of grace, does not deal with the lost but with the saint. Justification is God's saving act in dealing with a believing sinner. Sanctification does not produce salvation, but justification gives salvation. Justification is God's redemptive act of grace wrought in the nature of the sinner as he believes; while sanctification is the gradual unfolding of the redemptive benefits to the developing saint. Justification is the guarantee of sanctification; and sanctification is God's testimony and witness that He is faithful to His justification of the believer.

6:1

"Shall we continue in sin, that grace may abound?" Paul asks and answers the objection that he anticipates in some reader (See the first paragraph in 3:1). The possible objection arises from the last part of chapter 5 which might seem to prove what he denied in 3:8. It is true that the work of grace is mightier than the work of sin. But its greatness is in the deliverance from sin and not in the licensing of sin. The power of Christ's death is in His saving from sin and not in preserving in sin. Sin does not obtain grace for license; but faith obtains grace for the forgiveness of sin of any magnitude. (See the exegesis in 3:8.) There is plenty of grace for forgiveness of sins, but none for the propagation of sins.

τῇ ἁμαρτίᾳ (the sin). The noun is used rather than the verb. The question therefore is not shall we continue or remain in the practice of sin, but in the principle of sin. This does not license the acts of sin, but eradicates them by going to their source—the principle and nature of sin. The dative case denotes realm. Those justified can not, from the nature of sin and the nature of grace, live in the realm of both. Grace changed the nature of the believer so that he is no longer in the realm of the sin-principle. The practice of sin is foreign to the believer since he does not live in the realm of sinful nature. Grace delivered the believer from corrupt human nature. The delivered one does not remain in the sin-principle.

Grace abounds through faith and not through sin. Thus, sin limits grace rather than causing it to abound. Faith obtains multiplied grace for sin; but sin does not multiply the grace; and far less will grace multiply sin.

Grace abounds in removing sin, but never abounds in promoting sin. The death of sin does not give life to sin. The death of sin is not its resurrection. Sin does not gather strength from its death and destruction. The leading of sin captive does not establish the reign of sin. And that which establishes our righteousness does not make us bigger sinners; and that which makes us like God does not make us devilish.

Bankruptcy might reveal a man's mistake and lead him to make millions, but a man would be a fool to think of going broke that he might become rich, or to continue in bankruptcy that riches might abound. Neither do we continue in sin that the riches of His grace might abound. The philosophy as expressed in this folly is held only by those who are yet in the realm of the sin-principle and thereby strangers to the transformation by His grace. A life based upon such reasoning is contrary to Christian experience. The redeemed person does not want to sin. Assurance is no hindrance to right living. The wife being bound to her husband in love does not tempt him either to divorce her or to live as if they were divorced. The promise of God is no temptation for the redeemed to live as if there were no God. Grace came upon the condition that the sinner turn from sin in repentance and accept the righteousness of God. The abhorrence of sin is not to love sin. The penitent one turned from sin in the same attitude with which God condemns sin. Only as we embody His grace can we claim the fruits of it.

6:2

μὴ γένοιτο (let it not be, let it not come to pass, God forbid). See the notes on this expression in 3:4.

"We who died to the principle of sin, how shall we yet live in the realm of it?" Death to sin is set out in contradiction to living in sin. As Christ died for sin, so the believer died to sin when by faith he appropriated the death of Christ for his atonement in justification. "Died once for all," denoted by the aorist tense, is contrasted from "yet live in it." The believer dying to sin once for all assures the life he lives to be eternal. "Died once for all" precludes any lapsing back into death, and thereby is the guarantee of a continued life in the deliverance from the sin-principle.

The dead can not return to the old life. They are in a new realm, and do not practice the works of the former life. They do not promote their former businesses and occupations. This is the believer's experience when he died with Christ to sin. The believer being dead to the principle of sin and to the penalty of sin is thereby dead to the practice of sin. Being dead to sin and living in it are contradictory terms and exclusive realms.

6:3

$\H{\eta}$ (or) introduces the correct view in contrast from the false position. Paul offers baptism as a commentary on the Christian life. Baptism sets forth the believer's relation to sin, to the old self, to Christ, and to the resurrection life.

Baptism is first of all a burial. It is the burial of the body of sin that died with Jesus on the cross through faith. We were buried with Christ in baptism not in order that we might die to sin, but because we were already dead to sin. We do not bury living people, but the dead. Likewise, the believer is baptized, not to save him, but because he is already dead to sin, and alive to Christ; and he is baptized to proclaim publicly the inward work of grace.

Baptism is symbolical of the believer's having died in Christ's death. Baptism is an interpretation of the believer's experience in grace. Experience is exemplified in baptism. Thus, it has no meaning nor significance except as the believer's baptism. Baptism being based on experience in grace, death to sin, and living unto God rules out infant baptism and the seeker's baptism. The burial of a believer is the New Testament mode of baptism. The first meaning of baptism is death. Sin is consummated in death, and burial is the consummation of death.

The relation of death to the funeral is the relation of salvation to baptism. Baptism has no place nor significance except as the immersion of a believer. The Jewish error of circumcision is no more foreign than "infant baptism" and "baptismal regeneration." Faith, experience, and death to sin are essential to baptism. Baptism is valid only when the candidate has died to sin in Christ (6:1-5), but without meaning if the subject is not "raised . . . to walk in the newness of life" (6:4).

Believers died to Christ in His death, and not in His burial. This clearly reveals the absurdity of baptismal regeneration. The burial of Christ was not His death, but the exhibition of His death. Thus, baptism is not the death of the sinner, but is the symbolic consummation of the death of the believer, just as the funeral is the consummation of the dead.

6:4

This verse shows the second view of baptism which is a resurrection from the watery grave. We were buried to show that we had died to sin, and we are resurrected to publicly proclaim that we are alive unto God to live the resurrection life imparted in justification. (See the exegesis of 4:25.) As we died in the death of Jesus, so we live in His resurrection. The death is shown in the burial, and the life is exhibited in the resurrection. The death is shown in the immersion, and the resurrection is proclaimed in the emersion. Thus, baptism symbolically pictures the believer's dying to sin and living unto God. The immersion, the submersion, and the emersion historically picture the death, burial, and resurrection of Jesus.

The believer is more than dead to sin—he is alive to righteousness. He died with Christ, was buried with Him, and was resurrected with Him. He died to sin that he might live the resurrected life. The resurrection benefits are appropriated to us here in the earthly life. The guarantee of our final resurrection is that we are already living the resurrection life. We are the children of the resurrection, and fellowshipping in His resurrection as we wait for the resurrection of our bodies.

"Through the glory of the Father." This Scripture notes the glory of God that attended the resurrection of Jesus, and implies that the same manifestation of divine glory ought to characterize the walk of the Christian in his new quality of life. This is the chief reason why the saved can not continue in sin. In this idea is revealed God's estimate and standard of the resurrected life. The glory of God is the crowning of the resurrection life. Thus, the glory of the children of the resurrection brings them virtually to heaven. In the mind of God, there is very little difference between the initial time of salvation and its consummation in heaven. We are heavenly children, and can live only in accordance with our nature—a heavenly life. The children of the resurrection live a heavenly life unto the glory of God, and can never live under the dominion of sin. The two ideas are contradictory as to reason, impossible as to nature, and repulsive as to righteousness.

6:5

σύμφυτοι denotes implanted, united, grafted, being innate. If we have died with Jesus, we also live with Him. Since that death is consummated in a burial, likewise the life is consummated in the resurrection. Being dead to sin guarantees our resurrection, and the resurrected life is the final consummation of the death to sin.

The union with Christ holds throughout, both in death and in life. The graft is engrafted. It is supported by the life of the tree. And the life fluid of the eternal Tree of Life guarantees the eternal life of the engrafted. So as the believers died to sin once for all, likewise do they live the one eternal resurrection life.

6:6

"Our old man" denotes the unregenerate person of our past. We are said to have been crucified with Jesus, in order that we understand that the time of our dying with Christ was when He died for us.

καταργηθῇ is translated "done away," but literally means to work down, exhaust. Through the death of Christ, sin is powerless, impotent, sterile, barren, paralyzed, and rendered inactive. Sin has become an invalid, in order that it might no longer hold us in bondage to serve it.

τὸ σῶμα τῆς ἁμαρτίας (the body of sin). "The old man" denotes the unregenerate nature. "The body of sin" denotes the physical body as the instrument of sin, that is, the physical self as it is under the power and reign of the principle of sin. The genitive of "sin" denotes the nature of the body; and the article with "sin" denotes the mastery of sin over the body. And the "body of sin" is disabled in the crucifixion of the "old man."

6:7

The dead are said to be justified from sin in that they are no longer the servants of sin, nor the subjects of the penalty for sin. The dead owe no more obligations, debts, nor vows, as death is the full punishment of the guilty. Sin must release its grip upon the dead as if in a legal proclamation of acquittal. The law being unable to touch the dead man for his sins is a permanent acquittal, and may be correctly termed "justified from sin." It will be noted that Paul did not say justified "in sin," but "from sin." The former is never true, the latter is always true. The person who is dead to sin has no more connection with it. It is the sin-principle that is under discussion.

6:8

"Dying with Christ" guarantees our "living with Him." "We died once for all time," as the aorist tense denotes. "Believe" is in the present tense and denotes the actual reality of present faith. We have no English verb for "faith," so have to translate it "believe." It is faith that lays hold on the reality of the life with Christ. "Faith" is not a blind wishing for the best. Faith is knowledge, evidence, and reality. The knowledge of this faith is based upon the evidence of (1) our having died to sin once for all time, (2) our having died once for all with Christ, (3) our being resurrected with Him, and (4) our present experience in the reality of a vital living relationship with Christ in the present.

συνζήσομεν (we shall live with) is in the future tense. This does not mark the life with Christ as a future life merely; but denotes the life that is present to be continuous and eternal. The life with Christ is not held out to the believer as a future reward; but the present possession of life by faith is the assurance of the future with all eternity. The believer has eternal life here. The only life God gives is eternal; and we come into the possession of it by faith here on earth. The emphasis of this word is not that we live with the Person of Christ, but that we, now and eternally, live the life of Christ.

σὺν χριστῷ (with Christ) denotes vital union with the person of Christ. σὺν (with) prefixed to ζήσομεν (we shall live) denotes vital union with the life of Christ. The prefix σὺν (with) denotes a more vital and identical relationship than the preposition (σὺν). If we die with Him, He does the dying for us. But when we live with Him, His life is as much a vital part of us as it is of Him. He suffered the historical reality of our dying in substitution for us on the cross; but He imparts His indestructible and eternal life to us as the reality of our very own life. We do not personally participate in the historical reality of His death; but we do personally and vitally partake in the reality of His eternal life. Therefore, there is no distinction between the eternal life of the Savior and the eternal life of the saved; just as the life giving fluid in the vine likewise supports the branches.

6:9

εἰδότες (knowing). We have evidence that the resurrected Christ can never again die. Interpret this Scripture in the light of οἴδαμεν (we know) in the exegesis of 2:2.

The resurrection of Christ left death forever in the past and enters the future for eternity. We now see that we can not make distinctions between the life of Christ and the life of the believer. Thus, what is said of Jesus is likewise vitally true of the redeemed. Therefore, the believer having died to death once dieth no more forever.

6:10

Jesus died unto sin—once—momentarily, so to speak. But His life is an eternal living unto God. This is revealed in the static or eternal present tense. Jesus made one sacrifice of Himself, and then entered into the heavens with the blood of the perfect sacrifice to be repeated no more forever. Thus, by the one offering, He obtained eternal life for the believer.

6:11

λογίζεσθε (reckon ye) is imperative. Paul commands, not as a master, but upon the authority of their being dead to sin and alive unto God. Christ died once for the destruction of sin, so we died once for all unto the principle of sin. And as He dies no more forever, so are we to live eternally unto God in Christ Jesus. We died in His death; we live in His resurrection (See 4:25).

6:12

ἡ ἁμαρτία (the sin). See the exegesis of the same word in 6:1.

τῷ θνητῷ ὑμῶν σώματι (the mortal body of yours) denotes that physical part of us that is subject to death. Paul has proved that the principle of sin has no relation to the new nature of the believer. Here he exhorts the Christian not to let sin rule over that part of us which is mortal—subject to death. He has said that sin can not live in the believer's new nature. Here he urges that sin not be allowed to express itself through that part of us that is not yet redeemed. The redemption of the body will not be till the resurrection of the body. He does not say that sin resides in matter, but encourages that the physical body not be surrendered as instruments of the devastating tyrant of sin. Sin is not innate to matter, but the body is the most common instrument under the reign of sin. Sin does not find its rise in the flesh, though it finds in the flesh its most often means of expression.

ἐπιθυμίαις (lusts) denotes lust, desire, longing as coming from the seat of affection. See the notes on the same word in 1:24.

6:13

τὰ μέλη (the members). This denotes any functional part of man's nature—all the faculties of man, physical, mental, and spiritual.

ὅπλα (instrument, weapons). Sin is a monarch, mobilizing the members of the whole man as weapons of immorality to battle against God and His righteousness. The Christian is not to volunteer any member as a weapon in such a conflict. The believer's powers, ability, influence, personality, and body are not to become weapons of immorality, warring under the dominion of sin as a personified king.

ἀλλὰ (but) is the strongest conjunction, and marks the sharpest contrast between what they ought not to do and what they ought to do.

παριστάνετε (you present) . . . παραστήσατε (you present). This word means to present, yield, surrender, to place at the disposal of another. It carries the Old Testament idea of offering a sacrifice, and is the same word used by Paul in 12:1 as he said, "Present your bodies a living sacrifice." It carries the most plastic idea of receiving every impression and conforming to every mold, will, and influence. Every person yields and conforms to either sin or righteousness. And every one yields himself as a sacrifice either unto immorality or unto righteousness.

The first use of this word is in the present tense and imperative mood. The significance of the present tense is: do not keep on yielding unto sin, do not continue to yield, nor keep on yielding habitually, nor repeatedly at intervals.

The second use of this word is in the aorist tense and imperative mood. The aorist denotes an action as once for all time. The significance of Paul's entreaty here is that they by one decisive act present themselves once for all time in devotion to God. Such action is final in its decision—never needing repetition. The person who is thus presented is permanently situated.

In presenting one's self in one decisive act, most of the temptations of life are met triumphantly. Some have to reason, argue, and decide every Sunday morning as to whether they will go to church. It is ever an undecided question—ever, but never being decided. This question should be decided once for all Sundays, so that the question would never again arise for argument. The time to meet a temptation is before it comes. The person who meets his temptations separately, each as it comes, finds himself unprepared—yet ever inviting them by his defenselessness. By one resolute and decisive act present yourselves once for all time unto God, and you have barricaded against sin and prepared to meet sin without an argument. We must not parley with sin, nor argue with temptation, nor dispute and consider as to its dangers and offers, but rule over it without hesitation. Thus, sins, perils, and temptations lose their power when met before their existence by one decisive act of dedication unto God as once for all time.

"Neither present your members . . . but present yourselves." The members, the powers and faculties, of the person are employed in sin. But the real self, in addition to the members, is presented to God. The Christian may sin, but his deepest, innermost, real self abhors the deed. But in service unto God the Christian, in addition to his members, gives himself in his nature, and in the true reality of his inner Ego. We can not give ourselves unto sin, but we can yield our members to sin. We are to yield our members once for all with the soul that was saved once for all. According to this verse, the saved can not give the totality of themselves to sin, but only their members—the functional organs of their Ego. But unto God is given their members together with themselves. Thus, Paul distinguishes between presenting our members unto sin and presenting ourselves and our members unto God.

6:14

The reason for the preceding argument is that we are not lorded over by sin. This verse is also the summary statement of the above portion of this chapter, and the transition into the remainder of the chapter. "Ye are not under law, but under grace" is the negative and positive explanation of why sin is no more lord over us. "Sin shall not have dominion over you" and "ye are not under law" are the statement and explanation of the same idea. Sin is the monarch, the law is his strength. The one is king, the other is his regal authority. The power of sin is the law, and sin has lost its power in that we live under grace (1 Cor. 15:56). Living under grace is to be free from both the guilt of sin and the power of sin, from the corruption of sin and the penalty of sin. Sin reigns in death, law reigns in execution, grace reigns in life. There is no death nor execution in the realm of grace (See the notes on 3:31).

Paul concludes his argument proving that grace does not encourage sin. He has proven that we are dead to sin (6:2); that sin has been rendered powerless (6:6); that death is dead (6:9); that we are alive unto God (6:11); and that grace is reigning (6:14).

2. *The believer is dead to the practice of sin.* 6:15-23

6:15

ἁμαρτήσωμεν (shall we sin) is aorist subjunctive tense, and asks concerning the occasional sin in the absence of the life of sin. Shall we sin even occasionally in the future, since there is no law against it? Not living under law is not license nor "no law." Grace is a higher law. Law can make prohibitions, but it can not prohibit. Law penalizes the transgressor, grace prevents their being transgressors. Law warns of the danger, grace bridges the chasm. Law would convict, grace keeps the believer from the guilt. To break the law is not to supersede it; nor is the one under the law free from it; and to live in sin is not to live under grace. Grace perfects and supersedes law. The liberty in grace is not license to sin, but freedom from sin.

6:16

οἴδατε (ye know). See the exegesis of the same word in 2:2.

δούλους (servants). See the notes on this word in 1:1.

Every man is a servant of some one master. Everyone is under the supreme command of some one authority. Man can not serve two masters, nor render a divided obedience. Men do not serve strange masters, but their own. Man is the servant of the master to whom he renders obedience and service. The master has absolute power and authority in commanding him in subjection, "whether of sin unto death, or of obedience unto righteousness." The final subjection of the one is unto eternal death, while the obedience of the latter produces righteousness. Obedience to God does not give eternal life, but it produces righteousness, and the final goal of the justified is eternal life. We live in Christ, but we serve in good works. We do not obey to be saved, but we obey because we are saved.

6:17

The Christians of the church at Rome had been in servitude to sin, but that is past. They now render heart obedience to a new doctrine. "Heart" denotes the obedience as coming from the center and essence of their moral nature (See notes on "heart" in 1:21). The word "heart" is a challenge to serve God, not only as faithfully and as well as they did sin, but to serve Him from their moral nature; that is, that their moral standard of living shall be from the totality of their moral and spiritual understanding, emotion, will, intellect, personality, and activity. God demands that the service rendered to Him shall be moral.

The words translated "ye became obedient" and "ye were delivered" are both in the aorist tense, and carry the idea of once for all time.

6:19

ἀνθρώπινον λέγω (I speak as men). For notes on this word see 3:5. This verse is the repeated challenge to give themselves as completely unto righteousness as they had formerly served sin.

σαρκὸς (flesh) refers to the carnal nature of man, as it is prone to sin. The infirmity that it denotes is preeminently moral, then intellectual and physical.

τῇ ἀνομίᾳ εἰς τὴν ἀνομίαν is translated "to iniquity unto iniquity." The literal meaning of the word is "no law," and denotes lawlessness both from violation and contempt. The emphasis is not upon act, but upon the principle of lawlessness.

ἁγιασμόν (sanctification) is without the article in order to express the highest type of moral character. Sanctification must be understood as progressive and not instantaneous.

6:20

When they were servants of sin, they were free in regard to the possession of righteousness, that is, destitute of righteousness. And now that they are free from sin, they ought to be likewise destitute of sin. The article with "righteousness" denotes it as the righteousness of God and not of man; imputed and not personal.

6:21

Paul so skillfully words his question that it admits no answer. He asks, "What fruits did you have among the things that now shame you?" What are the values of the past life that so embarrass you now? Paul put the fruit in the past, but he recognizes the shame as ever present. God forgives us, but we never forgive ourselves. There is no forgiveness outside the grace of God. God freely forgives all sins unto the utmost, but the believer ever bears in his own consciousness the shame of his evil past. The embarrassment from past shame is one evidence of salvation. The wicked "glory in their shame" (Phil. 3:18), but the redeemed "glory only in the cross of our Lord Jesus Christ" (Gal. 6:14).

Paul does not name the occasions of their shame, nor does he permit their voices to reply, but only their consciences. He only makes the charge and leaves their memory and conscience to convict and torment in a painful silence of remorse. He does this in order to heighten their joys in the Lord and to emphasize their fruits in sanctification. Paul's refusal to enumerate some of their sins implies that their shameful deeds should not be even mentioned nor discussed, and never practiced since "the end of those things is death."

6:22

The preceding verse pictures the readers in their lost condition in the shameful past. This verse reveals them in the glory of their salvation, together with an intimation of their glory yet to be revealed in the life eternal. The two verses contrast the old life from the new. The old life is filled with occasions of shame, the new has the joy of fruit unto sanctification. The destiny of the former is eternal death, in antithesis to eternal life as the destiny of the righteous.

6:23

This verse is at once the woeful summary of one phase of this chapter, and at the same time it is the glorious conclusion of the redemptive element of the chapter.

ὀψώνια denotes pay, wages, rations, allowance. It denotes, not the salary of a laborer, but the allowance or rations to a soldier, such as bread, meat, and salt—that which sustains bare existence. Sin never pays well, but only enough to entice the sinners to keep working for the deadly wage. Sin only supports a bare existence. The hire that sin pays to its warriors is death. There is no deceit about their allowance. The sinners know that the wages of sin is death. Sin pays faithfully, promptly, and eagerly. But in the final analysis, the dying sinners do the paying. They pay the price of sin by an endless torment in hell. Some one has said: "When you work for God, He pays; when you work for the devil, you pay."

Death and sin are inseparably connected (Gen. 2:17; Isa. 1:31). Death and sin are essentially the same—only different stages of development. Death is the natural outgrowth and development of sin. Death is related to sin as penalty, wage, and justice. "Sin, when it is fullgrown, bringeth forth death" (James 1:15). Death is the consummation of sin. Death for sin is just, the worker deserves his wages, and hell is merited.

The devil pays wages; but he pays in his own coins, and they will not pass currency in this world, nor in heaven, but only in the devil's own territory—hell. The price of sin will not buy anything except death. It was natural and only fitting that the chief priests should buy a cemetery with the price of Jesus' blood (Matt. 27:3-10). The tragedy of their sin was heightened in their purchasing a cemetery. This was only indicative that they should pay the penalty of their sins in death. The price of sin will not buy anything except death. Every sin leads but to the grave. Every transgression leads but to the cemetery. The sin of Judas became cords for his execution. The desires of his sinful heart clamored for death, and were only satisfied in seeking refuge in death. He had chosen the wages of sin, and only death could follow. The wicked heart is truly "beating a funeral march to the grave."

Death is earned, reward is due, wages are merited, and death in hell is just. But "the gift of God" is contrasted

from "the wages of sin—death." Grace is not desert, nor
pay, nor wages; but grace is the gift of God abounding
where there is no merit. The sinner earns eternal death
for serving sin in the fight against God and His Kingdom
of righteousness; but God gives His servants eternal life
through Christ Jesus our Lord. Sin pays according to
justice; God gives according to grace.

3.   *The believer is dead to the power of sin.* 7:1-6

Paul is not flattering his readers, but merely says, "I
speak to men who know the law." Paul makes this statement to enhance the reader's understanding of the argument. The law is the power of sin (1 Cor. 15:56). The
statement that Paul makes is "that the law hath dominion
over a man for so long time as he liveth," but no longer.
This is best illustrated in the marriage vow. The wife is
bound to her husband as long as he lives, and both are
free from the other when either dies. When either dies,
the other is free to marry another. The one dying is
free from the marriage law, and that death liberates the
other party also.

Therefore, when the Christian died in Christ to sin, he
is thereby dead to the law. The law does not die, but it
has no authority over the dead. Therefore, law has no
reign over the Christian. The illustration changes from
nature to make a true example of the spiritual union with
Christ. In nature, it is the living party that is united to
another. But with the Christian, it is the dying party
that is united with Christ. The Christian dies to sin and
to the law, and is free from the law. Being free from
the law, the believer is at perfect liberty and freedom to
enter another union. The union with Christ is a permanent marriage. He will never die, and the law of Christ
is eternal, and gives eternal life to those who are bound
to Him by the law of life. Therefore, being bound to a
new husband, the believer serves in the new relationship.

II. THE BELIEVER'S RELATIONSHIP TO LAW
OR
INABILITY OF THE LAW TO SANCTIFY
7:7-25

1. The law is not sinful. 7:7-13.
  1. Law reveals sin. 7:7.
  2. Law arouses sin. 7:8.
  3. Law slays sinners. 7:9-11.
  4. Law is abused by sin. 7:12-13.

2. The law is abused by sin to prevent sanctification in believers. 7:14-25.
  1. Justification does not take all the sin out of man at conversion. 7:14-17.
  2. Justification does not give the daily grace for moral performance. 7:18-20.
  3. The conflict between the remaining carnal nature and that nature which is born of God is evident that sanctification is not by law, but from another source. 7:21-25.

Romans 7:7-13 was not given to prove that law can not save. That subject has been proven and settled in 3:21—5:21. The nature and office of the law is here briefly stated to prove that the inability of the law to sanctify is not due to its being sinful. Though the law is good, it still can not sanctify the soul. Its office is different, and its nature is contrary to sanctification. The law is not sinful; for (1) it reveals sin (7:7), and (2) it slays sinners (7:9ff). The pure law can not sanctify; for (1) it arouses sin (7:8), and (2) it is abused by sin to work evil (7:12f).

Does the Apostle interpret his own experience with the law or another's? In either case is it the experience of the lost or regenerate soul? Paul is relating his own experience with the law, in order to give an experiential interpretation of the nature and office of the law. Paul's experience is not singular nor peculiar, but is representative of the totality of those who have law-consciousness.

Romans 7:7-13 discusses the nature and office of the law, irrespective of its relation to the lost or saved. Paul writes this passage to prove that the law is not evil. If it were evil, it might kill the sinner, but would not condemn sin; it might arouse sin but it would not reveal sin; it might be an evil executioner but not a just one. This entire passage is true with reference to the unregenerate, as well as the regenerate, except that law can not kill the redeemed. Yet this does not change the nature nor office of the law with reference to the believer, even as expressed in this passage. For sin would take occasion of the law to kill the saint, if it were in the power of law and sin. The nature and office of the law is permanent, and does not change with the convert.

The nature of the law is unchanged with reference to the regenerate, as sin would slay the believer if it could. As far as the law is concerned, its relationship to the saint is identical with its relationship to the sinner; but as far as the saint is concerned, he is dead to the law. So the law does not change its nature with reference to the believer, but the believer's nature is changed with reference to the law. That which could not affect the change, can not perfect it; and the law being unable to justify, can not sanctify. Law becoming the executionary agency of sin unto death can not be the sanctifying agent in the life that is eternal. The nature of law would have to be changed to change its office.

Whether this Scripture applies to the saved or lost is an imaginary difficulty, and was never in the mind of Paul. He merely intended to show that the law could not sanctify because of its very nature and office. The emphasis of relation to law is always upon the transgressor, and therefore upon the unregenerate. This only carries Paul's point to defeat any false notion that law brings sanctification. Sanctification deals only with the regenerate. Therefore, both the unregenerate and regenerate are denoted when the passage is forced to its final application; the sinner is condemned by the law, and the saint is not sanctified by it; but in the mind of Paul, neither the lost nor the saved is considered, in that he only shows the nature and office of law, though good, to be contrary to sanctification. The emphasis of law is upon the lost; but the full designation of sanctification is upon the Christian. The emphasis of this Scripture thus is not upon law, but upon sanctification; and law is discussed only as to its inability to sanctify.

Romans 7:14-25 then shows why the law can not sanctify. The question of whether this Scripture is to apply to the unregenerate or regenerate is more acute in this passage than in the preceding section. One other question settled ought to answer this one. What is the subject of the whole passage from 6:1—8:39? Scholars agree that this is Paul's proof that his doctrine of justification by grace produces morals. Our term for this idea is "sanctification." Paul discussed justification from 3:21—5:21. Now he devotes chapters 6-8 to sanctification. Therefore, this passage must be understood as proving that law can not sanctify. This is the most accepted position, but even then some who take this position contradict themselves by saying that the subject of this Scripture is the unregenerate, as if the lost were the subjects of sanctification. Sanctification deals with the redeemed and not with the lost. It is for the justified, saved, and redeemed; and not for the condemned. Dr. James Stifler gives "The Law can not Sanctify" as the heading of this whole passage of 7:7-25; but he contradicts his captions as he heads 7:14-25 as "No man is Saved by the Law." Now, if the whole passage is on sanctification, then the major portion is not on justification. If Paul is talking about sanctification, then he is not talking about the inability of the law to save. If he is talking about the inability of the law to sanctify, then he is dealing with the redeemed. The person discussed is a subject for sanctification. Only the saved are sanctified. Therefore, the question is answered as to the person in this Scripture. It is answered in the subject matter of the Scripture (chapters 6-8)—sanctification; and in the candidate for sanctification—the regenerate.

Phillipi refers the "I" in 7:7-13 to the unregenerate and the "I" in 7:14-25 to the regenerate. Meyer marks this as inconsistent, and states that the "I" in both passages refers to the same Ego. They are the same Ego; and state a consistent experience with the law, from Paul's earliest law-consciousness to the present, as evident that law can not sanctify a redeemed soul. Paul does not dissect his experience nor break it up to denote part as of a lost and part as of a saved man. But he gives his life experience as a unit to prove the inability of the law to sanctify. If you make divisions of Paul's experience, you would find some of it before his conversion. But even that proves his point; and man's wrecking analysis neither illuminates nor harms the truth of Paul's statement—that law can not sanctify. And any Christian's lifelong experience will prove the same thing.

The struggles described in this passage are not those of the sinner, but the warring of two natures in regenerate man. Justification does not take all the carnal nature out of man at conversion. This is the work of sanctification, which is progressive. Paul waits till the eighth chapter to reveal the agent in sanctification. His duty here is to rid his readers' minds of the error that sanctification comes through the law. So he gathers his argument from the law being abused by sin in 7:12f to show that law, not only could not sanctify, but was abused by sin to prevent the sanctification of believers. This is shown first in 7:14-17 by revealing sin as it abuses the law in making sinful appeals to the yet remaining carnal nature in the justified one. The unsanctified believer finds himself being preyed upon deceitfully by sin, through occasion of law and carnal nature. These two natures strive for mastery. The carnal abuses the law to gain supremacy. The regenerate nature needs not to be servant to the carnal, when sanctification may be had for the growth of regenerate nature and for the purification of the carnal. Romans 7:14-17 pictures the unsanctified believer as having his carnal nature preyed upon by sin.

Romans 7:18-20 shows that the unsanctified believer has no power to execute the will of the new nature. In the former passage, we had the appeal of sin. There sin furnished the power to execute the evil will. Here we have the appeal of the new nature, but only the will is present; the power to execute it is absent. Therefore the only performance is on the side of the enemy.

Romans 7:21-25 expresses a sigh from the occasion of the conflict in 7:14-20. The conflict between the remaining carnal nature and that nature born of God makes evident that sanctification is not by law, and therefore must come from another source. "I thank God through Jesus Christ our Lord" is an intimation of the source of final deliverance and sanctification; it is at the same time a transition to the next chapter where deliverance is perfected, sanctification is secured, and union with Christ is consummated.

III. THE BELIEVER'S RELATIONSHIP TO CHRIST

8:1-39

1. Believers are free from condemnation in Christ. 8:1-11.

    1. Freedom from condemnation. 8:1-2.

    2. Destruction of sin. 8:3-10.

    3. Triumph over death. 8:11.

2. Believers are the sons of God in Christ. 8:12-17.

    1. The Spirit gives life to man. 8:12-13.

    2. This life is sonship. 8:14-16.

    3. This sonship assures an inheritance of God with Christ. 8:17.

3. The suffering of this world is not comparable to the future glory of believers in Christ. 8:18-27.

    1. All nature groans in its waiting for the glory of the children of God. 8:18-22.

    2. We also groan within ourselves, waiting for our adoption. 8:23-25.

   3. The Spirit also groans in intercession for us until the day of the glorification of the saints. 8:26-27.

4. Believers have the full assurance of complete triumph in redemption. 8:28-30.
   1. The universe in its minuteness is governed towards our redemption. 8:28.
   2. Our salvation has been made sure from eternity past. 8:29.
   3. We have present assurance of salvation. 8:30a, b.
   4. Our redemption has been made sure for eternity future. 8:30c.

5. The song of assurance in Christ. 8:31-39.
   1. God is for us in the substitution of Jesus. 8:31-32.
   2. None can criminate the character of the elect. 8:33.
   3. None can condemn those whom God justifieth. 8:34.
   4. None can separate us from the love of Christ. 8:35-39.
      (1) Satan's array of the evils of the physical world can not separate us from the love of Christ.
         a. Tribulation—external suffering.
         b. Anguish—internal suffering.
         c. Persecution—oppression.
         d. Famine—starvation.
         e. Nakedness—dire want.
         f. Peril—jeopardy.
         g. Sword—death itself.
      (2) Evils arising from the invisible world can not separate us from the love of Christ.
         a. Life and death—the two general states in which man is related to the invisible world.
         b. Nor angels—evil spirits of Satan.
         c. Nor principalities—the combined powers of evil spirits.
         d. Nor an unmentioned or unknown power.
         e. Nor things present, nor things to come.
         f. Nor height, nor depth—dimension contains no fear for the redeemed.
         g. Nor any other creature—any unmentioned or unknown opposing force.

1. *Believers are free from condemnation in Christ.* 8:1-11.

8:1

   This whole verse is an exclamation and a shout. It contains no verb. The negative is the most emphatic.

νῦν (now) is not temporal but conclusive; not momentary but summary; not of time but eternity.

κατάκριμα (condemnation) is without the article, and therefore the emphasis is general rather than specific, that is, it denotes any judgment rather than the final judgment alone. There is no condemnation from any cause, person, or source. There is no cause within us for condemnation, for we are redeemed by the blood of Christ. There is no person who can condemn us, for God has justified us. There is no source of condemnation, for we are dead to sin and to the power of sin—the law (7:1-6; 1 Cor. 15:56). Being in Christ, the believer is just as free from condemnation as is Jesus. Jesus would have to be condemned before those in Him could be condemned. This can never be. "Those in Christ Jesus" are as safe as heaven—as safe as deity. Paul does not multiply words to assure our safety. He lets Christ Jesus be our assurance and safety. The statement in simple form denotes the believer's absolute safety as needing no argument, nor proof. He lets the gospel as presented in the Epistle be the explanation of "in Christ Jesus," and lets this safety make its own silent plea for the believer's assurance. If any believer should ever be condemned, come into judgment, and go to hell, then the loss of that one believer would disprove the truth of this Scripture. This Scripture being true, no regenerate person has ever lost his salvation, nor been condemned in judgment, nor gone to hell. It being true, no erasure has ever been made in the Book of Life. God glorifies all those—without the loss of one—whom He justifies (8:30). Happy is the man who believes God's Word, and rests for strength in the glorious assurance that "There is therefore now no condemnation to them that are in Christ Jesus."

8:2

This verse tells how we are alive in Christ Jesus. It is because "the law of the Spirit of the life in Christ Jesus" has superseded the "law of sin and death." The believer has by faith ceased to be under the dominion of sin and

death, but is governed by the Spirit of life—the Holy
Spirit. This is the proof of the believer's safety, and is
both the ground and agent whereby "There is therefore
now no condemnation to them that are in Christ Jesus."
The believer does not live in the realm of the cause and
power of death—sin and law; but lives in the domain and
at the fountain of life—Spirit, life, and Christ. Being
emancipated from the law of sin and death, there is no
more condemnation forever. "Law" denotes authority.
Sin has no more authority over the believer, while the
Spirit has absolute authority and sole reign in the life of
the believer.

ἠλευθέρωσέν (freed, liberated, emancipated). This verb
is in the aorist tense and denotes once for all. The Christian was liberated once for all time, and that freedom is
permanent with eternity.

8:3-4

ἠσθένει (keeps on being weak). The imperfect tense denotes the continued weakness of the law. Its weakness
has been and will continue to be co-existent with the
weakness of the flesh.

Paul is not charging the law with any weakness as to
its purpose. He says the inability of the law was due to
our weakness and frailty. Law failed to gain obedience,
not because it was weak, but because we were weak. God
sent His Son both to condemn sin and to be obedient to
law; whereby in Him we have both deliverance from sin
and obedience to law. As He fulfilled all the requirements
of the law, so we fulfill the law in our lives by living
above it with Him and in Him.

Jesus came in the flesh in order to redeem the body
also, and to meet sin on the same equality as man, and to
meet sin in its own realm, and to condemn sin in human
flesh.

The incarnation of Jesus broke the dominion of sin as a
principle. Jesus was in the likeness of flesh, but was an
exception as to sinful flesh. Jesus was one exception as to
the universal dominion of sin. Sin therefore ceased to be

universal in man in Jesus' incarnation. Then the death of Jesus broke the power of sin with respect to its totality. The exception, of the one Man—Jesus, is to be made the exception of every one believing through the death of Jesus. Since Jesus became the one exception in His life, it is possible for all to be exceptions through His death. The fourth verse says that our nature becomes partakers in His victory to live His life in the Spirit.

8:5

φρονοῦσιν (to mind, to understand, to think, to agree with). They that are according to the flesh think the things of the flesh. They give their best thinking to the flesh. Their minds dwell on the carnal. They agree with the carnal. Their thinking harmonizes with the appeals of the flesh. The mind of the carnal man is fashioned according to his unregenerate nature. And his reasoning and judgment, especially on moral questions, are just as wrong as his heart. A man's reasoning grows out of what he is. Those who are fashioned according to the Spirit have an understanding of the Spirit. They think His mind. They agree with Him. They give their best mind and noblest thoughts to Him. To be spiritual is to follow the mind of the Spirit. To be wise is to know the mind of the Spirit. To be obedient is to do the mind of the Spirit. To have power is to be filled with the Spirit. To be Christlike is to live in the Spirit. "For he that soweth unto his own flesh shall of the flesh reap corruption; but he that soweth unto the Spirit shall of the Spirit reap eternal life" (Gal. 6:8).

8:6

The consequence of carnal thinking is death. The things that carnal nature sets its very being upon only bring death. "Death here can mean nothing less than the eternal death of the soul. But when the Spirit governs a man's mind and affection, he is led to the consummation of life with all the resulting blessings. (For notes on "peace" see

1:7). Thinking brings its certain reward. It does make a difference what one believes. Sincerity can not be substituted for the truth, nor for the mind of the Spirit. It is the mind of the Spirit that leads to life and peace.

8:7-8

These two verses take up only the darker picture as revealed in the two preceding verses, to tell why the carnal mind results in death. The mind of the flesh is hateful and odious, and hating and hostile towards God. It is rebellious towards God. The emphasis of the "enmity" of the carnal mind is not upon its rebellion, but upon its being odious; not upon its hating but its being hateful; not upon its opposing God but upon its contempt for God; not upon its action but upon its nature. This is shown in "enmity" being a noun rather than a verb.

θεόν (God) being without the article proves the above sentences; and denotes the foul nature of the carnal minded in its reaction, not against the personality of God, but against His character, essence, and nature. If the article had been used, it would have marked the opposition as being against the Person of God. The absence of the article denotes the nature of the carnal mind to be at enmity against the holiness of God. His character is assailed by the carnal. God's righteousness is attacked. The Greek denotes the personality of the carnal minded, and emphasizes the character of God. The whole nature and personality of the carnal is odious to the nature of God, but the Person of God is ever ready to save the carnal. His holiness is offended, but His Person is ready to give of His righteousness unto the vilest of His enemies, who repent and trust in the blood of Jesus. The Person of God is for the sinner, but the holiness of God can not tolerate the sin. The nature of either is odious to the nature of the other. The hateful nature is offensive to the loving nature of God. Carnal character is antagonistic to the righteous character of God. Therefore, from the nature of the carnal mind, it can not be subject unto the character of God. Such a subjection is impossible from the essential natures of the two. Therefore, God can never be pleased with those in the flesh.

8:9

"But ye are not in flesh but in spirit." The pronoun and its position, the emphatic negative, the strongest conjunction, the present tense, and the absence of the article from "flesh" and "Spirit," all go to frame the firmest denial of the flesh and the strongest affirmation to the Spirit, that inspiration could muster from the world's most perfect language. The power of the Greek is mobilized in this simple declaration.

εἴπερ (if, as in the case of fact) does not denote doubt, but a fact for each individual to appreciate. We are in the Spirit, since the Spirit is in us. We are at home in the Spirit, since the Spirit is at home in us.

οἰκεῖ (dwells) means to abide, not to visit, but to dwell at home, to administer, to govern. This denotes deep fellowship and unbroken communion in obedience to the reign of the Spirit. The Spirit is the host and not a guest.

As our relationship to the Spirit determines His relationship to us, just so does our relationship to the Spirit of Christ determine the relationship of Christ to us. Paul puts it in plain language. We are Christ's if we have His Spirit; but if one has not His Spirit, he is none of His. The Spirit of Christ and the Spirit of God are terms for the Holy Spirit.

8:10-11

If Christ is in the person, the body of that person is dead. The body of Christ arose from the very nature of the fact that there was no sin in Him. Likewise, the graves can not hold the bodies of the believers, because righteousness is life through the Spirit. As the little seed is germinated and resurrected by the warming of the sun, just so the grave can not contain the bodies that have been ransomed from the principle of death. Life

and righteousness can not but result in the resurrection
of the bodies, through the Spirit of Him that raised up
Jesus from the dead.

2. *Believers are the sons of God in Christ.* 8:12-17

8:12

Being free from sin, death, and flesh, we therefore are
not obligated to serve them in the flesh. Being delivered
from these, we are deeply in debt to our Liberator—the
Holy Spirit. This debt can never be discharged if we
live after the flesh. For to live according to the flesh, is
to die. The debt is partially paid by killing the deeds of
the body. This is the safety of the life. Either the soul
will die or the carnal nature; and if the soul lives then the
carnal must die. Paul does not say that the carnal nature
might kill the justified soul. Rather he says in verse 8:14
that the sons of God are led by the Spirit.

8:13

This verse reveals Paul's attitude towards the human
body. There have been three primary attitudes towards
the human body. One is that of the pagans, who worshiped the body, because of its beauty and strength. The
Greeks exalted the body in art and sculpture, and revealed every human grace in its fullness and beauty; they
developed the body to its maximum strength. Paul would
not worship any human body; but urges that the flesh be
regarded as dead. And a refusal to live for the flesh
would not permit one to worship a body.

There is also the pseudo-Christian attitude that regards
the body as the source of sin. These, therefore, reason
that the affliction of the body perfects the purity of the
soul; that the exhausting of the physical is the exalting of
the spiritual; that the subduing of the physical is the
liberty of the soul; that the starving of the body is the
food of the soul; that the lack of proper protection in
clothing is the pure linen of the righteousness of the

saints. The sin is not subdued in reducing the body to the invalid. Sin is not in the flesh, but in the nature, the inner self, the soul. The paralytic or invalid may covet, hate, or have a rebellious spirit and an unregenerate nature. An invalid may be lost. The body may be tortured to death, but the sin follows in the soul to an endless hell.

Paul's attitude is that of Scripture. God gave him this knowledge. It is expressed in "put to death the deeds of the body" (8:13) rather than the body. The body is to be purified but not by affliction. The purity of the body comes from living and not through torturing. The body is to be purged by the spiritual rather than punished by the physical. Righteousness comes from internal transformation rather than external conformity. Exhausting the body does not strengthen the soul. The reducing of the physical is not the abundance of the spiritual. Burning the body will not purge the soul. Cutting the body will not wash the soul. Nature is deeper than the flesh. Paul's position on our relationship to the body is most beautifully expressed in 12:1. It is sacred, not to be worshiped but sacrificed; not idolized but presented as a living sacrifice, holy, and acceptable unto God. The body is not to be tortured, but regarded as the home of the soul and of the Spirit. The body is not to be abused, but the sin of the flesh is to be denied. It is not to be tormented for purging, but to be sacrificed through the life of the Spirit. The body is not to be murdered but to be made alive in Christ Jesus; not killed but renewed through the resurrectional power of Him that raised up Jesus from the dead.

8:14

Paul is not basing salvation on obedience. He says that the sons will be led by the Spirit. The saints will be led. The believers will persevere. The leadership of the Spirit is not the source of salvation but the test. Obedience is not the source but the proof of life.

8:15

In justification, we received not the spirit of slaves but the spirit of children; not the spirit of fear but of boldness to the throne; not of rebellion but of prayer; not the spirit of servitude to a master but of fellowship with the Father. The next verse shows that the adopted sons are born children. The Spirit gives life (8:12f), and that life is to be the sons of God (8:14ff).

"Abba, Father" is far more than repetition in Aramaic and Greek. Often a bilingual person finds his prayers, exclamations, and expressions from his innermost soul to be uttered in his mother tongue. "Abba" has its rise in the tenderest emotions and thus has its expression in the language of Paul's childhood—the Aramaic. It expresses the deepest filial affection, and the most profound sense of sonship, together with the fullest recognition of the Fatherhood of God to believers. From the very nature of the expression being in two languages, it is thereby evident that God is the Father of the believer irrespective of nationality. This initial evidence is an anticipation of His being the Father of the nations. (See paragraph five in 1:14).

8:16

The witness of the Spirit is God's testimony that we are His. The testimony of the Spirit is God's answer to the filial cry, "Abba, Father." "Abba, Father" is the child's yearning upward; while the testimony of the Spirit is God's brooding over. The child cries, "Abba, Father," and God answers back, through His Spirit, "Yes, my child." The Spirit that enables us to say, "My Father," also testifies that God says, "My son." And heaven rebounds in testimony to the cry of the Father's child. Our regenerate consciousness recognizes Him Who begot us. The begotten know the Father. We have a son-consciousness that knows the Father by nature. The Spirit of God bears witness in company with our spirit that we are His children. This is the Father-consciousness in affectionate response to the son-consciousness of believers.

τέκνα (children) properly denotes little children. It denotes children as begotten, those of natural relation, children by birth. The children of God are born to Him, and are akin to Him by nature. The term is used in tenderest affection. υἱὸς (son) denotes more the legal relationship in addition to birth.

8:17

Being children of God, we are the heirs of God. Having been begotten of God, we are the sons of God, and Jesus is our elder brother. Therefore, being filial heirs of God, we are joint-heirs with Christ. Joint-heirs receive equally. We are equal heirs with Jesus. We do not heir through Him but with Him. This denotes the character of the title, the certainty of the inheritance, and the quality of the possession. The character of the title is divine, the certainty of the inheritance is in our being joint-heirs with Christ, and the quality of the possession is heavenly.

The inheritance of the children is just as certain as is that of Christ. The title held by every believer is just as safe and secure as is the title of Christ. In an inheritance of joint-heirs, the heirship can not be broken with one heir without breaking every title with reference to all the heirs. The title of Christ can not be broken. Therefore, no title can be broken with reference to any other joint-heir. The inheritance is equally safe to every joint-heir. The faithfulness of the Father who promised, the certainty of the inheritance to the Divine Son, and the equality of the joint-heirs are grounds for absolute confidence in eternal assurance.

3. *The suffering of this world is not comparable to the*
   future glory of believers in Christ. 8:18-27

8:18

λογίζομαι (I reckon). See the notes on this word in 3:28.
Paul does not say that the calamities of this world
weigh less than the glory of the next; he says the sufferings of this life weigh nothing in comparison to the future
glory. All the weight is on the other balance; and all
the values of life are on the other side. Life is to be lived
with reference to the future. Suffering is to be patiently
borne in the hope of glory.

The sufferings and afflictions of this world are not to be
considered in relation to the future glory reserved of God,
to be revealed in the saints. εἰς ἡμᾶς does not denote
"towards us," but "in us." This is the correct interpretation in that the preposition (εἰς) is used with the accusative plural of persons. The highest glory of God is in
redemption, and that glory shall be expressed in us,
in our nature, and in our partaking of God's character.
We shall be like Him—there is no higher glory. God can
not give anything better than Himself. Union with God
is the highest glory of both God and saint. This glory
is so dazzling that tribulations lose their visibility under
the transparent light of the expectation.

8:19

ἀποκαραδοκία (earnest expectation) is compounded from
three words meaning "off from," "head," and "to look."
The expression denotes anxious yearning with a forward
reach of the head, to look with outstretched head, to eagerly thrust the head forward in earnest expectation. This
is the way nature is yearning for the revelation that is to
be exhibited in the sons of God. Nature can not relax nor
rest until the children are glorified. Creation can not be
at peace until the sons are blessed in the presence of
Prince of Peace. The article with God emphasizes the
Person of God, Who will reveal the glory of Himself in
the whole personalities of the sons. The article with
"sons" emphasizes personality.

8:20

Creation was made non-resultant; not willingly but unwillingly; not as a just reward but as an unmerited curse; not for nature's guilt but for man's corruption (Gen. 3:17ff; 4:12). All Nature was marred by the pollution of sinful man. The subjector was not Adam but God. The middle voice of ὑποτάξαντα (subjected) denotes volition, will, and consciousness. This is evidence that God subjected nature rather than Adam, who would have been an unconscious subjector.

8:21

The subjection of creation has been accompanied with a divine intent towards a deliverance. The curse was not permanent but promissory. Nature "possesses in the feeling of her unmerited suffering a sort of presentment of her future deliverance" (Godet). The present condition of nature is not its original state nor its final one.

8:22

The whole creation groans in travail for a new life, that is, for deliverance from its curse. Creation is faulty from the ruin of man. Man has defiled whatever he has touched. Nature crumbles under his hand. Man's sin put the thorns on the roses (Gen. 3:17ff). His sin makes the lamb fear and groan for peace with the lion. Even the teeth of wild beasts do not decay except in captivity. Pneumonia never attacks animals except as they are domesticated or held captive by man.

History is but the sin of the nations and the record of the ruins of man. History is little more than a war record. Crumbling cities are the monuments of man's hands. Wherever man has labored there are seen the heaps of ruins to his memory. There is nothing so pure on earth but that it has been polluted by man's corruption. Soon after we saw the morning light of creation, midnight darkness terrified the fallen souls. And those who were to grace the beautiful garden became homeless, murdered and murderer, and vagabond in the earth; and sorrow and sin began to multiply exceedingly.

8:23

And we who are Christians, who have the firstfruits of the Spirit and absolute assurance of a full harvest of the final glories, also groan in our spirits as we wait out the time for the redemption of our bodies in the resurrection.

8:24

But let none despair, for hope is in the very nature of our salvation—we were saved in hope. (See notes on "hope," 5:2). We were not saved upon the grounds of what we could see, but in faith as we trusted the word of God. Our very redemption, of life from death, is contrary and impossible as to the frailty of human evidence. We trusted to the impossible in the resurrection of a dead soul. The case of ἐλπίδι (hope) may be either locative, instrumental, or dative; and may denote in hope, by hope, or for hope. It would be exceedingly interesting to find out in heaven that this one word is in all three cases. The three cases are true to our experience. We are saved in hope, the saved are sustained by hope, and they are living for hope. The nature of our salvation essentially embraces the whole of the three ideas.

8:25

Patience is therefore native to hope. Patience is not a surprise to him who trusts in a promise and who hopes in the unseen. Sight does violence to hope and renders faith impossible. So patience is in the nature of faith, and hope is the essence of our salvation. Fretting is not hope; impatience is not trust; anxiety is not faith. Hope produces patience, and patience is the assurance in hope. Therefore, our patience ought to exhibit trust, to magnify faith, and to glory in the assurance of hope.

8:26

συναντιλαμβάνεται (he takes hold on the other side together with). The middle voice places special emphasis
upon the Spirit as acting. "The Spirit Himself takes hold
on the other side together with" us and helps us to pray.
The Spirit prays with us. Though we become speechless
from being overwhelmed or from natural inability and in-
firmities, yet the silent, unuttered prayers are borne to
the Father by the Spirit, in groanings that can not be
articulated by reason of great grief or much anxiety. God
reads our speechless prayers in the groanings of the
Spirit. The creation, the redeemed, and the Spirit, all
are in groanings for the consummation of our salvation.

8:27

And God, Who knows the secrets of the hearts, also
knows the unutterable words and the Spirit. He, Who can
read the grief of a broken heart, can also understand the
groans of the Spirit.

4. Believers have the full assurance of complete triumph in redemption. 8:28-30

8:28

This verse does not mean that what happens is best.
Paul does not say that all things work for our comfort,
ease, health, or prosperity. Sin can never be justified with
this Scripture. Sin is never good nor best. Evil is never
appropriate. (See the exposition of 3:8). If the article
had been used with πάντα (all), it would have denoted the
totality of events as affecting our good. But πάντα (all),
without the article, denotes the essence of all things to be
destined for our eternal good. The essence of all things
denotes all things in their true nature, real value, and
destined purpose.

Thus πάντα (all) here denotes the essential of all things
to be destined for our eternal good. The totality of essen-

tial things is summed up in the next two verses: foreknowledge, predestination, calling, justification, and glorification. While some occurrences are evil, yet they can
have no weight in thwarting the good whereunto we were
preordained. Our election is grounded in eternity past,
and is consummated in eternity future, and time and
creation are only subservient means to eternal ends. God
has ordained that nothing shall prevent our being glorified, and He has predestinated us unto eternal life. Therefore, all creation and all eternity are governed towards
the perfection of our redemption. Our salvation grew out
of eternity in predestination and is unfolded in eternity
in glorification. God governs the universe for a redemptive purpose. This is a redemption centered universe.
Consummated redemption—glorification—one far-off divine event to which the whole creation moves!

8:29

προέγνω (foreknew). God is omniscient and knows everything. He has known everything from beginning.
Nothing is a surprise to God; nor does He ever come
into possession of new knowledge. Thus, God knows all
people. But this word means more than an intellectual
knowledge. It means that God knows some in a special
way, in a redemptive relationship, in grace, in life from
eternity. This is the initiative of our salvation. Redemption has its rise in God and not in man.

προώρισεν (preordained, predestined). Those whom God
foreknew in a redemptive relationship are then predestinated to be made in the likeness of the inner character of
Christ. "Preordained, or predestinated" means that God,
in eternity past, determined and purposed to save those
whom He knew or elected. When God purposes the salvation and ordains it in eternity, nothing can thwart the
omnipotence of God. Predestination is the assurance that
the elect will be conformed to the image of the Son, Jesus
Christ. The believers' predestination is based upon what

God is, and not upon any merit in man. That is, salvation grew out of God and not out of man.

8:30

ἐκάλεσεν (called). This call is more than a general gospel invitation to men to be saved. This call does not come to all who hear the gospel. It comes only to those whom God foreknew and predestinated. But the call comes to every one of those—"whom He foreknew, he also foreordained . . . them he also called . . . them he also justified . . . them he also glorified"—ever without the loss of one.

The emphasis of this call is in eternity rather than in time; in predestination rather than in the historical gospel appeal. (Study "called" in 1:1 and 1:5). The tense of this divine act is aorist, and denotes once for all time. Paul makes no distinction in the time element in the predestination, calling, and glorification. These five mighty verbs are all in the aorist; the first being second and the others first aorist. The nature of glorification and its relationship to predestination does not disprove the unity of the time element as denoted in the aorist tense; but all are harmonized with the tense, in that the whole of God's redemptive dealings with man have been culminated in eternity past to co-exist in eternity future. He Who redemptively knew us in eternity past also foreknew us in glorification in eternity future. In the mind of God and in the act of God, man can not separate between eternity past and eternity future, nor distinguish between the time element in predestination and glorification, nor separate God's initial redemptive act from the consummation of redemption.

Whom God foreknew, them He preordained to be identical with the character of Christ. Then He called them to make them like Christ. The justification is the transformation of the sinner to the character of Christ; and glorification is the consummation of the change. In the experience of the man of time, the divine acts operate

timely and periodically; but in the mind of God, His acts
are one, eternal, finished in eternity past, and consummated for eternity future. The tense of completed action
denotes glorification as evident, as sure, and as real as
predestination. In the mind of God, the unborn elect are
already glorified. He Who "chose us in him before the
foundation of the world" (Eph. 1:3f) foreknew us in
glorification. He Who preordained our redemption, likewise in the same act preordained our glorification as the
culmination of His redemptive foreknowledge.

5. *The song of assurance in Christ.* 8:31-39

8:31

"Since God is for us, who is against us?" The common
interpretation of this Scripture is that if God is on our
side, we can win any fight against any or all others. This
interpretation immediately takes the low plane of physical force. The correct interpretation hinges on the word
translated "for" which denotes "substitution." This interpretation immediately exalts the subject matter to the
loftiness of the eighth chapter. "Since God is for us in
the substitution of His Son, who can touch us?" Having
a substitute, the believer is out of the picture, and can
never be touched in that he has a substitute.

The fundamental idea in ὑπὲρ (for, above), according to
New Testament usage, not root meaning, is substitution.
Romans 8:29f enumerates the fivefold way in which God
exhibits Himself to be for us. They are: foreknowledge,
predestination, calling, justification, and glorification. God
is for us from eternity past to eternity future. ὑπὲρ (for)
denotes these five things as provided through the substitutionary death of Christ. The death of Jesus is the proof
that God is for us. God is for us in the substitutionary
death of His Son. Since God is our Substitute, no one can
be against us. The substitutionary work of the dying
Christ is His atonement (8:34). The substitutionary

work of the living Christ is His intercessory office (8:34). Not only was He our Substitute in death, but He Himself is our Substitute now and eternally. Therefore, Satan can never attack our souls. Everything, from the beginning of time through the death of Jesus to His eternal intercession, vividly manifests God as for the redeemed in substitution. We are saved by substitution. We are safe through substitution. The reason no one can ever be against us is because we have a Substitute.

As God substitutes Himself for the believer, then He can no more be against the believer than He could rebel against Himself. He could no more cast the Christian off than He could cast off Himself. To deny the believer would be to deny Himself. To be against the Christian, He would have to be against Himself, and thereby He would cease to be God. Therefore, His existence is the guarantee of our existence. The impossibility of God's denial of Himself is our guarantee of the impossibility of His denying us. Not to be for the believer would be to oppose Himself. For the Substitute to be against the one whose place He took would be contrary to the nature of the Substitute, an impeachment of His character, and a division of His Own nature. He would have to bring judgment against Himself, before He could condemn the one for whom He is the Substitute. God being the Substitute, if there were any judgment, the Substitute must bear it. The believer can not be touched since he has a Substitute and has passed from condemnation into life (8:1; John 5:24).

To condemn the one for whom He is the Substitute, God would have to rescind His substitutionary action in the atonement. The death of Jesus can not be rescinded. That action is historical, and history can not be rescinded. The death of Jesus is not only an historical fact, but Christ, in the mind of God, has stood "the Lamb slain from the foundation of the world" (Rev. 13:8, A.V.)—and eternity can not be rescinded. The heavens and the earth and all things therein were created for a redemptive purpose,

and creation can not be rescinded.   His substitutionary
death could not be rescinded without rescinding the historical atonement, God's eternal purpose, His eternal will,
even all eternity and all creation. Substitution is according to His wisdom and purpose—His nature. Failure to
regard His substitution would be the breakdown of His
character, revolt in His own nature, and collapse of His
immutability.

If the Substitute could be annulled with reference to
one believer, then the sacrifice would be declared null
with reference to every believer. For if God is inconsistent with Himself with reference to one believer, He
could not be consistent with Himself to another. For in
the death of Christ, God deals with Himself and not with
the believer. God's attitude towards the believer is His
attitude towards the Substitute, that is, His attitude towards Himself. God could not be untrue to the believer
without proving false to the One substituted. God is the
Substitute and must be true to Himself. And the believer
is safe as long as the Substitute is efficacious. Therefore,
the regard for Himself will be His regard for the believer. And His consistency with the believer will be measured by His consistency with Himself. So His self-con-
sistency is the assurance of His eternal substitution.

The danger of the believer's soul does not lie with
Satan; but his safety lies with God. The security of the
soul does not depend upon the failure of Satan but upon
the grace of God. Our safety is in our Substitute. Instead of the devil dealing with the believer, he has to deal
with the Substitute—God. Instead of God dealing with
the believer, He likewise has to deal with the Substitute
—Himself. The devil can not deal with God. And God
is morally bound to deal consistently with Himself. Then
"Who can condemn?" is asked and answered three times
in verses 8:33-35. The conclusion, therefore, is that condemnation is neither the question nor the state of condition. "God justifieth"; wherefore, justification is the
only truth to be stated in the matter, and when that is

said, all is said—that is final. The reason no one can be against us is because we have a Substitute. "There is therefore now no condemnation to them that are in Christ Jesus" (8:1)—no one against us; for there is eternal justification in the substitutionary death of Jesus Christ.

A saintly old woman lived in the highlands of Scotland. She had been an invalid for many years. Her young pastor often visited her—more for his own good than for hers. One day he sought to test the strength of her faith by asking, "Suppose that, after all your praying and all your trusting, God should cast you off at last—what then?" The old woman raised upon her elbow and said, "Eh mon, is that a' the length ye got to yet? Why mon, God wad be the greater loser. Poor Nanny wad lose her soul, to be sure, and that wad be a sad loss indeed, but God wad lose His character. He knows I've just hung up my soul and all my hopes upon His own precious promises; and, if they should be broken, the whole universe wad gang to ruin"; and then, sinking her voice, she added, "For God wad be a liar."

8:32

ὑπὲρ ἡμῶν πάντων denotes "in substitution for each of us" (cf. 8:31). Since God delivered up His only begotten Son as our Substitute, He will give us all things. τὰ πάντα denotes the whole universe of things. We receive all things in Christ.

8:33

"Who shall lay anything to the charge of God's elect?" "Who is he that condemneth?" It is most evident from the personal pronouns in these questions that the archenemy of Christians is personality. Creation is subservient unto the Christians; only personality can war against personality. Saints do not fight matter, but personality, powers, and principalities.

ἐκλεκτῶν (elect). The absence of the article reaches the height of its significance with reference to this word.

Its first significance here is that it denotes essence, quality, and character. The genitive adds its full qualitative power to heighten the character of the elect. If the article had been used, it would have emphasized personality. The absence of the article renders the verse, "Who, what personality, shall criminate the character of (the) elect of God, 'while' God is declaring them righteous?" Satan would make his attack on character. It is satanic, even in man, when the attack is made on character. Satan knows that he can not reach the person of the elect, since they have Christ as their Substitute (8:31). This question does not ask, if Satan can ever touch the souls of the redeemed. That question was settled in 8:31. This verse says that Satan can never impeach the character of the elect. The reason he can not impeach our character is because the courts of the tribunal of heaven have declared us righteous in the character of God. The unimpeachableness of our character, in which we defy the principalities of hell, is not personal for man to boast, but we glory in that we are clothed in the righteousness of God, which is unimpeachable (2 Cor. 5:21).

There is yet another "shouting ground" preserved by inspiration in the absence of the article from "elect." There is no verb for this noun. The presence of the article would have denoted a specific election at a definite time. The absence of the article denotes a definite election at an indefinite time, and refers the election back with God in eternity. No point of time can be marked as the moment of the election of the elect. They have always been elected. There was never a time in all eternity when they were not (the) elect of God. Our names have been written in the Book of Life from the foundation of the world (Rev. 13:8) ; and this expression denotes eternity. "He chose us in Him before the foundation of the world" (Eph. 1:4).

8:34

"Who is he that shall condemn?" is asked in order that the acquittal of the believer might again be magnified. Any condemnation by the devil is unthinkable, and is therefore neither mentioned nor considered. Christ will not condemn where God acquits. Deity is not divided. Christ can not condemn, for He is dead to the believing sinner. Shall the living Christ condemn? No! He is making intercession for us, at the right hand of God. Christ's relation to our sin is that of death; and therefore, He can not condemn us. His relation to our salvation is that of life manifested in the resurrection and intercession, that is, redemption and preservation; and therefore, He will not condemn us. Condemnation is not even the question. He died for our atonement, was raised for our justification, and intercedes till the consummation of our redemption in glory. The work of Christ can not make our redemption any more sure in heaven than is the assurance already secured.

8:35

The personal pronoun is an implication of the devil in the satanic mobilizing of the forces of nature, together with forces of the evil spirits against the Christian. No one, implying Satan, can accuse us before our God (8:33). No one can condemn us (8:34). No one can separate us from the love of God in Christ Jesus (8:35). Satan may array all the evils arising from this world, but they shall neither quench Christ's love for us, nor diminish our love for Him (5:3f).

"Tribulation, or anguish." See the same words in 2:9. διωγμὸs (persecution). The tribulation and anguish bring persecution. The things that are suffered bring a like response in the attitude of the public. Thus, persecution follows hard upon him, who is bowed down under the weight of tribulations and depressed in anguish by the pressure of affliction. Paul speaks out of personal experience. He says, concerning others: "Are they ministers of

Christ? I more; in labors more abundant, in stripes above measure, in prisons more frequent, in deaths oft. Of the Jews five times received I forty stripes save one. Thrice was I beaten with rods, once was I stoned, thrice I suffered shipwreck, a night and a day I have been in the deep; in journeyings often, in perils of waters, in perils of robbers, in perils by mine own countrymen, in perils by the Gentiles, in perils in the city, in perils in the wilderness, in perils in the sea, in perils among false brethren; in weariness and painfulness, in watchings often, in hunger and thirst, in fastings often, in cold and nakedness." (2 Cor. 11:23-27.) And "in Damascus ... through a window in a basket was I let down by the wall, and escaped" (2 Cor. 11:32f).

λιμὸς (famine). Persecution drives to famine and nakedness. Famine and nakedness denote the end of peril and jeopardy. The sword is symbolical of death. And these words were wrought out on the anvil of Paul's experience. "Even unto this present hour we both hunger, and thirst, and are naked, and are buffeted, and have no certain dwelling place, and labor working with our own hands: being reviled, we bless; being persecuted, we suffer it; being defamed, we intreat; we are made as the filth of the world, and the offscouring of all things, unto this day" (1 Cor. 4:11ff).

It is difficult for some to feel a consciousness of Christ's love while they are suffering. They feel so unworthy of His love that they take afflctions as expressions of His wrath. God loves, not because we deserve it but because we are in Christ. The love of God is denoted, not by the things we suffer but by what Christ suffered for us. His love is not revealed in the material blessings, nor does affliction denote the absence of His love; but the cross is the eternal exhibition of His love for us. The love of God is not to be measured by our surroundings but by our redemption. We would not prove the love of God by the times but by eternity.

8:37

We are more than conquerors, we are over-victorious, we gain a surpassing victory, through Him that loved us. Victories are won nowhere except in Christ. But in Him all victories are won. For He conquered every enemy, and we only have to take the vanquished foe.

8:38

πέπεισμαι (I am persuaded) is in the perfect tense which denotes permanency. Paul is persuaded for all time of the impossibility of any evil arising from the invisible world, that can separate us from the love of Christ. Paul has stated that no peril from the physical world could harm our relation to Christ (8:35). Now he turns to the perils of the invisible world. Life and death are the two general states in which man is related to the invisible world. Neither can separate us from the love of Christ. Whether in life or death, the redeemed are the objects of His love (cf. 1 Cor. 3:22). "For whether we live, we live unto the Lord: and whether we die, we die unto the Lord; whether we live therefore, or die, we are the Lord's" (14:8).

"Nor angels, nor principalities" can only denote the evil spirits and their combined powers. Paul is not talking about heavenly ministers and powers as they serve the redeemed souls. He is mentioning personalities and powers of the invisible world, in their futile efforts to separate us from the love of Christ. "Nor powers" is added to include any other power that is unmentioned or unknown.

Paul exhausted the invisible perils in "personality and principalities." Now he considers them in relation to time and eternity. "Nor things present" in time, "nor things to come" in eternity can affect our relation to Christ.

8:39

"Neither height, nor depth," denotes no dimension of space in which there exist or ever will exist, either personalities or principalities, that can separate the redeemed from the love of the Redeemer. He adds "nor any other creature" to include any opposing force unmentioned.

This Scripture is final in its exhausting of the futility of the opposing forces of the Christian, and it is sublime in its assurance of the eternal love of God in Christ Jesus our Lord. The Christian, who is so weak in himself, triumphs over worlds and principalities in Christ. We may be weak and poor unworthy creatures in this world, but we live and move, and have our being in Him, Who has subjected every thing to His government, and Whose footstool is the earth (Ps. 110:1; Matt. 22:44; Heb. 1:13).

THE THEODICY

9:1—11:36

V

THE NATIONAL REJECTION OF ISRAEL
9:1-29

1. Paul's heart is breaking over Israel's rejection. 9:1-5.

1. He states his grief under oath. 9:1.
2. The statement of his grief. 9:2.
3. His grief would love and sacrifice. 9:3.
4. The glory of those for whom he sorrows. 9:4-5.

2. The principle of exclusion has co-existed all the time with selection. 9:6-13.

1. This is sustained by Scripture. 9:6a.
2. There are two Israels—natural and spiritual. 9:6b.
3. Isaac only was chosen from all Abraham's seed. 9:7.
4. In Isaac, God chose, not those by flesh but those of promise. 9:8.
5. This is shown in rejection of Esau, and selection of Jacob. 9:9-13.

3. The exclusion is according to divine justice. 9:14-29.

1. God does not wrong one by showing mercy to another. 9:14-16.
2. God is just even in hardening men's hearts. 9:17-18.
3. The potter has a right to fashion the clay according to his will. 9:19-21.
4. God has a right to select vessels unto destruction or unto glory. 9:22-23.
5. God therefore has a right to select vessels unto glory from either Jews or Gentiles. 9:24-26.
6. By this right, God retains a remnant in all ages. 9:27-29.

Paul would first assure Israel of his love for his kinsmen, and of his deep grief in their lost condition, before exhibiting before them their national rejection from the Messianic Kingdom.

He places himself under oath of truth, of conscience, and of the Holy Spirit, in expressing his great love by

211

means of his deep grief in the rejection of Israel. His great sorrow is stated in the second verse and measured in the third verse. Paul would be willing to be condemned to eternal death, if it were possible and if it would bring Israel to Jesus in salvation. He would be willing to suffer Israel's doom, if only all Israel might thereby be saved. This was the spirit of Moses in Exod. 32:30-32. This statement shows the source of Paul's grief to be love; and love would express itself in sacrifice. The glories of Israel are enumerated in verses 9:4f. This glory is an intimation of what Israel might be, and a conviction of how far he has fallen short (9:1-5).

In 9:6-13, Paul shows that the exclusion of Israel is not an impossible thing, nor is it a recent transaction. The principle of exclusion has coexisted with selection from the beginning of Israel's national existence. This is not inconsistent with God's selection of Abraham and his seed. For from all of Abraham's children only Isaac was chosen, while the others were excluded from even national blessings. And from the National Israel, God chose only the Spiritual Israel. "For they are not all Israel, that are of Israel" (9:6). And from Abraham's covenant seed, God chose only the faithful, that is, his true seed were those by faith. And from the children of even Isaac, God chose only those who were the sons of promise. This is shown in God's selection of Jacob and His rejection of Esau, before their birth. This selection and rejection were based wholly upon God's right of choice, and not upon what the twins were in themselves. God acted with reference to them, before they were born, and therefore before there was any personal good or evil, upon which the selection or rejection might be based.

9:14-29, show that God is just in His selections. God can not be condemned in His selections, nor accused in His rejections. No lost person deserves any favor. God is obligated to no human. All deserve the worst. Then God's selection of one is an act of mercy and not of merit. Is God unjust in giving one mercy and another justice? God does not wrong one by showing mercy to another. The lost man can not accuse God for his being lost nor condemn Him for saving another. The one is saved in mercy; the other is lost in justice. And God is righteous in meting out justice to one or mercy to another. The holiness of God demands justice, while the atonement of Jesus provided mercy. Those obtaining mercy can only glory in God, and those obtaining due reward can not blame God.

So far is God from wronging one by being merciful to another, that Paul says in 9:17f that God is not unjust in doing the very opposite—even hardening of men's hearts. Paul again cites them to Scriptural proof. The outstanding example of God's hardening the heart is that of Pharaoh. Pharaoh first hardened his own heart, and then God hardened it. God's hardening of Pharaoh's heart does not indict God nor acquit Pharaoh. (See the last paragraph in the notes on 1:24).

Then Paul seeks to illustrate the sovereignty of God by the familiar business of the potter (9:19-21). The clay is obedient to the potter's mold rather than rebelliously accusing the master-mind as is the wicked practice of man. The potter makes temple vessels; and from the same lump, he may fashion an urn for the ashes of the dead. From the same lump of clay, he may make either a vessel of beauty or one of ruggedness; one may be crude and another the embodiment of the skill of his science.

Likewise, God has an inherent right to fashion from the same flesh some unto glory and others unto destruction (9:22f). And He has the right to select those vessels unto glory from either Jews or Gentiles (9:24-26). God is not obligated to save all of any race irrespective. Nor is His grace limited to any family of people. His grace is to every one that believeth, whether of Jew or Gentile, Greek or Barbarian, wise or unwise,—or black or white, red, or yellow. By this inalienable right is God able to retain a remnant in all ages (9:27ff). If God did not choose some, none would ever be saved. If God did not choose them, they would never choose Him. If God did not take the initiative in salvation, none would ever come to Him. This right of God guarantees an unceasing remnant in Israel. Left to Israel, there would be no Spiritual Israel (9:29). But left to Him, Who is just and also merciful, there will always be a seed in Jacob and a remnant in Israel.

VI

ISRAEL ALONE IS TO BLAME
FOR THE REJECTION
9:30—10:21

1. **The cause of Israel's rejection. 9:30-33.**
   1. The Gentiles were accepted upon faith-righteousness. 9:30.
   2. The Jews were rejected because of their work-righteousness. 9:31-33.

2. **Paul reassures them of his love by his grief. 10:1.**

3. **Faith-righteousness contrasted from law-righteousness. 10:2-13.**
   1. Jewish zeal is not according to truth. 10:2-3.
   2. Christ is end of law unto righteousness to every believer. 10:4-13.
      (1) Moses did not intend the law to save but to establish a standard of conduct. 10:5.
      (2) The faith-righteousness does not demand the impossible. 10:6-7.
      (3) Righteousness of God may be had by simply believing God. 10:8-13.
         a. The possibility of righteousness is so near the Jews. 10:8.
         b. Believe the word of God as you have received it. 10:9-11.
         c. They may be saved by calling on His name. 10:12.
         d. Invitation is to whosoever will—Jew or Gentile. 10:13.

4. **The Jews have had full opportunity to believe the gospel. 10:14-21.**
   1. They have heard the gospel. 10:14-18.
   2. They have understood God's pleadings. 10:19-21.
      (1) God plead with them through Moses. 10:19.
      (2) God plead with them through Isaiah. 10:20.
      (3) God made personal pleas to them. 10:21.

In 9:1-29, Paul discussed the sovereignty of God in salvation. He showed how man's salvation has its initiative in God rather than in man; and how man's salvation and Israel's spiritual acceptance have their basis in God rather than in the subjects.

In 9:30—10:21, he discusses man's personal responsibility and guilt in being lost, and Israel's personal blame in being rejected. He attributes salvation unto God; but holds the lost to be guilty for their rejection. He makes no effort to harmonize the sovereignty of God and the free moral agency of man. Both are true and basal principles in theology; they never conflict and always run parallel. These two ponderous doctrines made no strain on Paul's faith, and he perhaps never imagined they should cause others to stumble.

Unto God is the glory for the salvation of the remnant, but Israel is to blame for his national rejection. Though God saves, He is not to blame for any being lost. Israel alone is to blame for his rejection.

The cause of his rejection will become more apparent when contrasted from the ground of Gentile acceptance (9:30-33). The Gentiles never had a revealed, spiritual law. They never had a system of morality, even though some followed their moral conscience. A law-righteousness had always been foreign to their knowledge and practice. Having no system of righteousness, they were unhampered in accepting the system best fitted for their woeful need—a faith-righteousness. This was the only method whereby the Gentiles could attain unto righteousness. In it, they found the righteousness of God and the acceptance of God. This faith-righteousness produced the true nature of God in even Gentiles, in contrast to legal morality in the Jews. The Jews could see the Spirit of God working in power, transforming unrestrained Gentile depravity into flaming evangels, for the turning of many hearts unto God. And the Jews marveled that the Spirit of God was poured out upon the Gentiles. They had to believe in Gentile acceptance, though they would not dare to admit it even to themselves. And what they inwardly feared to believe, they outwardly manifested in hate and complaint.

The Jews did not experience that inner personal communion and fellowship with God. Their religion had grown into a burdensome ritualism, grievous to be borne. Their religion did not have the vital heart touch with God that made it joy, peace, and life. Perhaps some wondered if God had forsaken them. Paul makes the woeful declaration that the Jews are without God, and therefore are rejected by Him. They have not the righteousness of God, therefore they have no righteousness.

The difference is not in God, nor in the two races of people, but in their method of obtaining righteousness. The Gentiles, having no righteousness, obtained the righteousness of God by grace through faith (9:30). The Jews, seeking to establish their own righteousness by law, rejected the righteousness of God which they might have had through faith. The difference in the acceptance of one race and the rejection of the other is found in faith and absence of faith respectively. To cling to law is unbelief; to turn to God for salvation and righteousness is faith. Faith obtains God's righteousness, law obtains wrath. Faith lays hold on life, law brings death. Faith brings the gift of God, law brings the wages of sin—death (6:23; 1 Cor. 15:56). Righteousness is obtained in the one, guilt is retained in the other. The former finds the righteousness of God, the other seeks the righteousness of self. In the first is acceptance, in the second is rejection.

In 10:1, Paul reassures his people of his love by proof of his grief. Then he enters in 10:2-13 upon the contrasting of the faith-righteousness with law-righteousness. He says the Jews have a zeal, but not according to truth (10:2f). They are religious but it does not produce fruit. God is not in their worship. God does not live in their lives. Their law-works have choked out spiritual living.

Then Paul shows the Jews how to live the law in which they have so far fallen short (10:4-13). Christ met the law for us, and the only way we can meet the law is in Christ. "For Christ is the end of the law unto righteous-

ness to every one that believeth" (10:4). Christ is the
last word in the law; He is the fulfillment of all laws; He
is the perfection and consummation of law. And the absence of the article from "law" shows Him to be the end
of any law, every law. The absence of the article would
throw emphasis upon the quality that meets the law.
Christ has the character to transcend any qualitative
requirement in law. He is the end and consummation of
law, in every respect. The Jews can meet their law by
faith in Christ—but nowhere else.

Moses gave a protective law but not a saving law
(10:5). He said one would live by the law he performed.
The violated law of Moses gave no haven nor refuge, but
justice and penalty. Any Jew has broken enough of the
Mosaic Law to be lost, even if it were redemptive. To
offend in one point is to be guilty of breaking all law
(James 2:10). But the law was never intended to save.
God has only one means of salvation. Grace is the only
possible way whereby God can save a sinner. Even God
is limited by Himself, by right, and by finality; He is
conditioned by His own character.

Faith-righteousness does not demand the impossible
(10:6f). The righteousness is easy, simple, full, and final.
This may be had so easily; salvation is potentially so near,
in that the word has already been planted in their hearts
(10:8). The righteousness that years of toil could not
obtain may be had in a moment by faith in the gospel as
they have heard it. The simplicity of faith may stagger
some. It is so easy and simple. Faith is just to trust God
(10:9ff). When man believes with his heart, he will want
to express his new life (10:10). The confession does not
save, but expresses salvation. The words of the mouth do
not save; but faith from the heart saves. This is not a
new doctrine, for Joel 2:32 saith, "Whosoever shall call
upon the name of the Lord shall be saved" (10:13). And
this Scripture extends the gospel invitation to "whosoever
will"—Jew or Gentile.

Paul devotes the remainder of the chapter (10:14-21) to prove that the Jews had ample opportunity to have believed the gospel message. Their rejection is for their unbelief, but they can not plead the absence of the message (10:14-18), nor the lack of understanding (10:19-21).

They have heard the gospel message about Jesus (10:14-18). Paul admits that no one can call upon Christ nor believe in Him for salvation without having a knowledge of Him (10:14). "How beautiful are the feet of them that bring glad tidings of good things" (10:15) proves that they have been visited from of old (Isa. 52:7) by the true way of life—first with reference to the promised Redeemer, and now with "Behold the Lamb of God, that taketh away the sin of the world" (John 1:29).

Nor can the Jews plead a lack of understanding (10:19-21). They well know God's pleadings with his people, from Moses, through the prophets, and even to the present weary pleadings. God told them through Moses (Deut. 32:21) that He would exclude them in favor of a foolish (Gentile) nation, when they return to Him (10:19). Then God witnessed His saving power among the Gentiles (Isa. 65:1) even from of old (10:20). Then Paul sums up God's personal pleadings (10:21) by quoting Isa. 65:2, "All the day long did I spread out my hands unto a disobedient and gainsaying people."

VII

THE FINAL RESTORATION OF ISRAEL

11:1-36

1. There is a remnant left in Israel. 11:1-10.
    1. Paul is a Jew and belongs to the remnant. 11:1.
    2. God has never cast off the elect. 11:2a.
    3. There was a remnant in the days of Elijah. 11:2b-4.
    4. There is a present remnant in Israel. 11:5.
    5. The remnant consists of those in grace, and not those of works. 11:6.
    6. The elect were accepted; the others were hardened. 11:7-10.

2. The rejection of Israel is to issue in their restoration. 11:11-32.
    1. The purpose of Israel's rejection. 11:11-15.
        (1) To admit Gentiles to salvation. 11:11-12.
        (2) To provoke Israel to follow God for salvation. 11:13-15.
    2. Israel's rejection ought to enrich Gentile fruit. 11:16-24.
        (1) The engrafted must not glory in the graft but in the stump. 11:16-21.
        (2) The graft is not necessarily permanent. 11:22-24.
    3. The Jews are the beloved of God, and shall be saved when the Gentiles are full and rich in Christian living. 11:25-32.

3. The doxology. 11:33-36.

The two preceding chapters might indicate to the Jews that God is unfaithful to His promise to Israel. Paul defends God's promise by presenting two facts: (1) there is a remnant left in Israel (11:1-10), and (2) the rejection of Israel is not to be permanent but is to issue in a restoration (11:11-32).

God promised Israel that He would be their God, and that they should be unto Him a peculiar people forever. Israel was God's people in a sense unlike the possession of

220

any other. Israel understood this covenant to be eternal, and God meant the same. Then has God proven unfaithful to His covenant? Has God broken His promise?

Paul says there is yet a remnant in Israel (11:1-10). God has not cast off all of Israel. Paul gives his personal testimony of both his genealogy and Christian experience, to prove that God is saving Jews, just as fast as they believe (11:1). None could be a better example than Paul of what Judaism and Christianity can do for a person. None had purer lineage nor a clearer "title to mansions in the sky." He says he is an Israelite and that God has not cast him off. He attributes his acceptance to his faith in Christ. So God has not cast off all Israel.

In 11:2a, Paul makes a courageous statement, the truth of which startles the Jews. First it seems that Paul contradicts himself; then conviction grips through truth and guilt. He makes the bold statement that God has never cast off His people, the true Israel, those whom He foreknew—the elect. God could not cast off the elect and be morally consistent with Himself (re-read exegesis of 8:31). The salvation of the elect is just as certain, as is God. Nothing rests firmer in the economy of God. This statement says that God has never called any people His own except the elect. It further denotes that He will consummate the salvation of the totality of the elect—without an exception.

This Scripture thus implies that those cast off were not of the elect and therefore were never His chosen people in grace. National Israel is cast off; but Spiritual Israel was never cast off, and can never be cast off. National Israel is not the elect Israel.

The rejected National Israel was so near a hundred percentage of Israel, that the elect Israel was reduced so low numerically that she could not retain the spiritual leadership of the world. Though Israel was too few in number to be the world leader in Christianity; yet there has ever been even until now a seed in Israel. To human eyes the remnant might seem to be few or none, as it seemed to

Elijah (1 Kings 19:10; Rom. 11:2b). As God told the lonely, despairing Elijah that He had a remnant of seven thousand elect yet in Israel (11:2b-4), so has it been even till now, that God has preserved a seed in Israel—the elect, those whom He foreknew, and whom He will never cast off (11:5).

In 11:6, Paul explains that the elect rest in grace and not in works. "Grace" denotes the elect of God. "Works" denotes the rejected, National Israel. In "grace" and "works" is implied both the eternal election of the believer and the personal responsibility of the unbeliever. Paul at once speaks of the election of those in grace and of personal belief or unbelief, as distinguishing between the elect and the rejected. Paul exalts the sovereignty of God and the freedom of human choice. These two fundamental doctrines are in perfect harmony and never conflict. Those in "grace" are the elect; those in "works" are rejected because they willed to be out of grace.

Verses 11:7-10 say that National Israel never obtained that which he sought. He sought righteousness, life, and salvation. The elect reach that happy goal through faith in Christ. The others were hardened in their sins. This is natural. The redeemed live near God both in tribulations (5:3f), and in the love of God (5:5-11). But the lost stray in prosperity, and complain and blaspheme in times of distress and peril.

God is said to harden men's hearts as He did with Pharaoh. But God never hardens the godly heart. God is never the first to harden any heart. When God hardens a heart, it is always after the person has already hardened his own heart. And when God hardens a heart, He holds the sinner guilty of the hardening. God never hardens a heart in the sense that He makes a man sin. But He hardens men's hearts, just as He gave up the wicked Gentiles to the evil lusts of their vile affections. He gave them over to their own sins. He released restraint that they sin in the liberty of their evil choice. (See the notes on 1:24). The lives of the elect exemplify their God, and the lost grow harder. Each rejection of Christ hardens the unbeliever a little more. No lost person has a tender heart. They have hard hearts that are rapidly growing more callous. No person can turn from Jesus without doing serious detriment to his moral character. Each rejection of Jesus plunges the unbeliever deeper into the night of darkness. There are only two lines of reaction to Jesus. The one is to accept His mercies, the other is to spurn His blood. The one is to respond to His love, the other is to withdraw through hate. The former is to love Him, the latter is to hate Him. The one is to trust Him, the other is to reject Him. The one is to become tender with Him, the latter is to harden against Him. The first is to become like Him, the latter is to rebel against His righteousness. The former is to increase in Christlikeness, the other is to increase in hardness.

There is a higher purpose in the fall of Israel than his rejection. By Israel's stumbling, salvation is brought over to the Gentiles, and, in turn, the conversion of the Gentiles is to stir the Jews to jealousy, and thereby hasten the return of Israel (11:11). Shall the restoration of Israel provoke the Gentiles to be jealous of their spiritual leadership? It ought not. "If their fall is the riches of the world, and their loss the riches of the Gentiles; how much more their fulness" (11:12). Whatever blessings were forfeited to the Gentiles by the Jews, the benedictions of the restored Israel shall be manifold more in Gentile riches. "For if the casting away of them is the reconciling of the world, what shall the receiving of them be, but life from the dead?" (11:15). And if the fruit of Israel is holy when her branches are cut off, what glorious fruit must grace her branches when the holy root shoots forth in the strength of the Tree of Life (11:16).

At the present time, however, the branches are Gentile, being grafted where the Jewish branches were broken off (11:17). And the spiritual fruit of the world is borne on Gentile branches. But the Gentiles are not to boast themselves that they bear the spiritual fruit of the world.

Pride will be held in check, as the Gentiles remember that though they bear the fruit, yet they are borne by the ever living Jewish stump (11:18). Gentile branches are not trees, but branches grafted into Israel's stock where Jewish branches were broken off (11:19). So the Gentiles were ingrafted from necessity and not from preference. The Gentile branches remain, not by their pride nor by virtue of their place, but by their faith; and the Jews were broken off for their unbelief (11:20). It is here inferred that the Gentile branches shall be broken off only for unbelief, and that the Jewish branches will be ingrafted at the moment of their faith in Jesus. For since God spared not the Jews in their unbelief, He will no more spare Gentiles in their unbelief (11:21). And if He would graft unnatural branches for their faith, how much more readily will He graft the natural branches for their faith (11:21, 24)?

The Gentile graft is not permanent. It exists by reason of faith and the goodness of God; and may perish by reason of unbelief and the severity of God (11:22). The Gentile branches shall continue to exist so long as they respond to God's nurturing, otherwise they also shall be cut off (11:22). The Jews also shall be grafted in when they believe in Jesus, "for God is able to graft them in again" (11:23). It is far more natural to graft the tame olive branches into their own root than it is to graft wild olive branches into a tree contrary to their nature (11:24). If God will do the contrary thing with the wild branches, how much more will He do the natural thing with the true branches?

In verses 11:25-32, Paul says the fruit, the fulness, the riches of the Gentiles shall be the salvation of Israel. The emphasis of πλήρωμα (fulness) is qualitative rather than quantitative. When Gentile Christians are full of fruit, full of His grace, rich in Christ, this shall lead the Jews to trust the Gentiles' Saviour as the Jewish Messiah. Gentile salvation has not yet convinced the Jews of its genuineness. When Gentile Christians live like Christ, then shall both Jews and Gentiles come into Israel, and those from afar shall see His light and shall come for His salvation.

The joy of the anticipated salvation of Israel flooded Paul's heart, and his soul sings its doxology in heavenly rapture and ecstasy unto the glory of God. "O the depth of the riches both of the wisdom and the knowledge of God! how unsearchable are his judgments, and his ways past tracing out! . . . For of him, and through him, and unto him, are all things. To him be the glory for ever. Amen." (11:33-36.)

PRACTICAL

12:1—15:13

VIII

THE BELIEVER IN SPIRITUAL RELATIONS

12:1-2

1. The presenting of the body. 12:1.
   1. It must be a whole sacrifice.
   2. It must be a living sacrifice.
   3. It must be a holy sacrifice.
   4. It must be an acceptable sacrifice.
   5. This makes it a reasonable sacrifice.

2. The presented person must be free from the fashions of the age. 12:2a.

3. The presented person is transfigured through a renewed mind. 12:2b.

Read again the exegesis of 8:13 for the three preeminent views of the body. Paul's Scriptural view might well serve as an introduction to this section.

παρακαλῶ (I beseech, call up by the side of) is the verb for the noun translated "Comforter" in John 14:16, 26. This is one of the tenderest expressions in all the Bible. It carries the idea of a brother who lovingly and pleadingly goes up by the side of another brother and places his arm around the brother's shoulders to comfort, to bless, or to plead.

οὖν (therefore). There is the shout of victory in this conjunction. It carries all the weight of the eleven previous chapters. It denotes more than a connection of the two divisions of the Epistle. It means more than a conclusion. It is an accomplishment, new heights, a victory.

ἀδελφοί (brethren) denotes blood kin, and is the tenderest word expressing the closest relationship. Paul is not blood kin to the members of the church at Rome, except that they are redeemed and washed in the same blood—the blood of the Lamb, Jesus. They are brothers in Christ.

οἰκτιρμῶν (mercies) is used in the plural to denote the abundance of His saving grace. These mercies were named and discussed by Paul in the earlier portion of the Epistle. They are the mercy of God as expressed in the revelation of sin, the mercy of atonement, justification, sonship, sanctification, union with Christ, life in the Spirit, the hope of Israel, and glorification. These mercies are the arguments for presenting their bodies.

παραστῆσαι (present) means to present, yield, surrender, to place at the disposal of another. It carries the Old Testament idea of offering a sacrifice. It carries the most plastic idea of receiving every impression and conforming to mold, will, and influence. This word being in the infinitive form denotes purpose, aim, motion towards. The aorist tense urges that the bodies be presented once for all time, one decisive act, one resolute presentation of the bodies as a sacrifice, so that the act will never have to be repeated. In this connection read again the exegesis of 6:13.

In the word "present" is the idea of complete or whole sacrifice. A partial sacrifice was unknown and unthinkable to the Jews. Likewise, the whole of the bodies is to be presented upon the altar of sacrifice. The mouth may sing His praises, but the feet must walk in His way. The holy fires of God never come down upon a partial sacrifice, but only upon the whole. Likewise, neither do the holy fires of evangelism flame in the lives of those who are partially surrendered, but upon those who are wholly yielded.

"A living sacrifice" is the thank-offering and not the sin-offering. This expression marks a new distinction for the sacrificial idea in the minds of both the Jews and Gentiles. This expression carries the highest idea of self-surrender. The bodies of saints are to be presented in contradistinction to the prevalent sacrificial idea. The

Jews knew only of a dead sacrifice. To the Jewish mind, to sacrifice meant to die. Living through sacrifice was the essence of their offering, but this they did not consider. So Paul's words were strange in their ears, as he taught living by sacrifice and in sacrifice.

However, there was in the Jewish sacrifice a basis for the idea of "a living sacrifice." A Jew might live a hundred miles from Jerusalem. He could choose between two methods for obtaining a sacrifice. He could either buy an animal in Jerusalem, or if too poor to buy one, he could drive one from his home. This would be a living sacrifice.

ἁγίαν (holy). With reference to the slain animal, this word would denote clean, perfect, no blemish, no blood clots. The victim was slain for the altar. It may yet be rejected as a fit sacrifice. A priest, with a sharp knife, cleaves between the joints and into the marrow (cf. Heb. 4:12f), to see if there be any inner imperfections. When the sacrifice passes the keenest inspection, it is marked "holy." So the believer's body is a "holy" sacrifice, as it is morally presented unto God. The holy fires fall only on the holy. The body must be morally clean. Sin prevents the fires of God from burning richly in the heart and life. The fire consumed the dead sacrifice, but the living sacrifice is purged and refined in the fires of the Holy Spirit.

εὐάρεστον (acceptable) denotes well pleasing. A sacrificial animal might be offered in its entirety; it may be perfect internally and yet be rejected. A holy sacrifice may not be acceptable. Its acceptableness depends upon the offerer. Cain's sacrifice would not have been accepted, if it had been of blood as was that of Abel. Cain's heart was as wrong as his sacrifice. No sacrifice is acceptable, except as the heart and life of the offerer is acceptable. The offerer must first be acceptable before his sacrifice is acceptable. "Bring no more vain obligations; incense is an abomination unto me; new moon and sabbath, the calling of assemblies,—I cannot away with iniquity and the solemn meeting. Your new moons and your appointed feasts my soul hateth; they are a trouble unto me; I am weary of bearing them. And when ye spread forth your hands, I will hide mine eyes from you; yea, when ye make many prayers, I will not hear: your hands are full of blood. Wash you, make you clean; put away the evil of your doings from before mine eyes; cease to do evil; learn to do well; seek justice, relieve the oppressed, judge the fatherless, plead for the widow" (Isa. 1:13-17).

> "For Thou delightest not in sacrifices; else would I
>   give it:
> Thou hast no pleasure in burnt-offering.
> The sacrifices of God are a broken spirit:
> A broken and a contrite heart, O God, thou wilt not
>   despise."   (Ps. 51:16f.)

All of a person's prayers, songs, works, and services are rejected, except upon the ground that the offerer is accepted. All of a person's sacrifices are but an abomination and a stench in the nostrils of God, except that the offerer is well-pleasing unto God.

τὴν λογικὴν λατρείαν ὑμῶν (your logical service). The article marks the sacrifice, as the only logical service and as the only Christian sacrifice. Thus to present the bodies is logical and reasonable. λατρείαν (service) is not the work of a slave, but the sacrificial ministry of a priest. We are to present our bodies in priestly service. In this expression, Paul rises to the height of true priesthood. The believer is the priest of his own soul—ministering, not in temple but in the Spirit. This word condemns ceremonies and ritualism in religion, and exalts spiritual service which comes from spiritual living.

The ox is driven to slaughter. A logical sacrifice is a surrendered, voluntary, and yielded one. The soul is the chief value, so it is only logical to yield the body also, which is the lesser value. The soul has been intrusted to God, so it is logical to surrender the body also. The man is the Lord's, so the members of the man ought to go with the man.

μὴ συνσχηματίζεσθε τῷ αἰῶνι τούτῳ (Be not fashioned with the age). This is in the imperative mood. αἰῶνι denotes the "age" and not the "cosmos." Do not live for the age but for eternity. Do not live like the worldly people. The age is not the pattern for the Christian life. The Christian must let Christ be his model for Christian living, and not the age. When a Christian fails to deliver the message of the ages, he will become conformed to the spirit of the age. All people conform either to the Spirit of the ages, or to the spirit of the age.

This word properly refers to the changing customs and styles. The Christian is not to exhaust his spiritual strength on the passing fashions of a sinful age. The Christian is not to sacrifice right living for the latest dress. He is not to value customs more than The Commandments. He is not to prefer "good taste" to good sense. The correct dress is the pure linen of the righteousness of the saints. "Good taste" is to delight in His word day and night. "Being correct" is to be Christlike. Many people measure their lives by the fashions of the day. They think a person acceptable as he or she meets the requirements of society; pleasing as they embody the fashions; correct as they fulfill the standards of the age; good as they meet the expectations of the fashionable. The fashionable man can never have power. The fashionable woman is never spiritual. A fashionable age is not the standard nor the goal for Christians, but to be fashioned for the ages.

"But be ye transformed" is another imperative. Paul is not commanding as a master but as an authority. This is the same word as was used in the transfiguration of Jesus. "The fashion of the age" and "the transfiguration of the Christian" is the height of antithesis. When Christians present their bodies, deny the examples of the age, and are transformed in Christ's transfiguration through a new type of thinking, then shall they know and "prove what is the good and acceptable and perfect will of God."

IX

THE BELIEVER IN SOCIAL RELATIONS
12:3-21

1. The right use of spiritual gifts. 12:3-8.

    1. Hold the gifts in humility and sobriety. 12:3.
    2. The diversity of gifts. 12:4-5.
    3. The diversity of gifts comes by the grace of God in proportion to the faith of the believer. 12:6-8.

2. Moral and spiritual injunctions for the Christian life. 12:9-21.

    1. Love. 12:9-10.
    2. Service. 12:11.
    3. Christian traits. 12:12-13.
    4. The Christian among enemies. 12:14.
    5. The Christian among the sorrowing. 12:15.
    6. The Christian among other Christians. 12:16.
    7. The Christian among the public. 12:17-20.
    8. The Christian and sin. 12:21.

Paul urges the Christians to be grateful for their God-given gifts rather than proud (12:3a). The endowment of divine gifts ought to produce humility, graveness, and sobriety (12:3b). We have many members of our body (12:4). They are highly valuable but not in duplication. Likewise, a high value of gifts lies in their diversity rather than in their multiplicity (12:5).

In 12:6, Paul says that God gives the gifts in proportion to His grace, and that we use them in proportion to our faith. Then in 12:7f, he urges that whatever gift a man has, to apply himself to that responsibility. The implication is that each should exercise his own gift, and not be jealous of another's gift.

In the remainder of the chapter, Paul gives some moral

and spiritual injunctions for the Christian life (12:9-21). Let love be sincere (12:9a). Then he adds that love must be moral, and that moral love will react against sin with the same vigorousness with which it clings to the good (12:9b). Hating sin and loving goodness is not repetition of words, but the negative and positive statement of a Christian's experience. A man's love for righteousness is measured by his hating sin. He who is congenial with sin must be sinful by nature. The hating of the one is essential to the loving of the other. In 12:10, Paul states that moral love is not selfish, but prefers the brother above self. The implication is that it is not love unless it is moral. Then he gives one verse to a brief, yet exhaustive statement on service, "In diligence not slothful; fervent in spirit; serving the Lord" (12:11). The statement is in the same breath with "in love of the brethren, be tenderly affectioned; in honor preferring one another." It is thereby inferred that only love will serve in these characteristics.

Paul next brieflly discusses some vital Christian traits (12:12, 13). Hope is the predominant element in our Christian experience. Assurance is the essence of hope, and the predominant earthly fruit of hope is joy and patience. Patience is therefore native to hope. Patience is not a surprise to him who trusts in a promise, and who hopes in the unseen. So patience is in the nature of faith, and hope is the essence of our salvation. Fretting is not hope; impatience is not trust; anxiety is not faith. Hope produces patience and patience is the assurance in hope. Therefore, our patience ought to exhibit trust, to magnify faith, and to glory in the assurance of hope. And while we are patiently waiting for the consummation of our hope, we are to be "continuing steadfastly in prayer; communicating to the necessities of the saints; given to hospitality" (12:12f).

In the remainder of the chapter, Paul discusses the Christian in his relation to various phases of life. He first mentions the Christian among enemies, saying, "Bless them that persecute you; bless, and curse not" (12:14).

Then he sets out our attitude towards the sorrowing: "Rejoice with them that rejoice; weep with them that weep" (12:15). 12:16 is to characterize our relationship among other Christians. The Christian in public is discussed in 12:17-20. The Christian is never to return evil for evil. He must live honorably before all men; and as far as he is concerned, he must be at peace with all men. He is never to avenge—that would be usurping God's right. God can be righteous in punishing sinners, but man can not righteously avenge his transgressors. Rather bless the offending person by serving his fundamental needs in life. Returning good for evil will break his evil spirit.

Paul's last injunction regards the Christian's relation to sin. His relationship to sin is to be that of conqueror rather than that of its victim. Goodness is the weapon for the victorious fight (12:21).

X

THE BELIEVER IN CIVIC RELATIONS

13:1-14

1. Government is a divine institution. 13:1-7.
   1. Lawless citizens are lawless towards God. 13:1-2.
   2. Government is for the good of citizenship. 13:3.
   3. Governmental wrath upon lawlessness is the agent of God against evil doers. 13:4.
   4. Subjection to law is not only safe, but right. 13:5.
   5. Taxes grow out of conscience. 13:6-7.

2. Love is the fulfilling of law. 13:8-10.
   1. Love fulfills the law. 13:8.
   2. Love keeps the commandments. 13:9.
   3. Love always blesses his neighbor. 13:10.

3. Good citizenship and moral conduct are enhanced by the approach of our consummated salvation. 13:11-14.
   1. Consummated salvation is nearer than it was. 13:11.
   2. Live the heavenly life as the eternal day is now breaking. 13:12.
   3. Walk as children of the light. 13:13.
   4. The day robe is the Lord Jesus Christ. 13:14.

Paul counsels that every soul should be a law-abiding citizen, for law is divinely ordained (13:1). The lawless citizen is likewise rebellious towards God (13:2a). Submission to God is submission to law and order with reference to man. Lawlessness is consistent with itself in any relationship. And submission and obedience are permanent throughout all the relationships of a surrendered life.

There has never been a government, whose law was the safety of the evil doers. All governments have been for the terror of the evil and the protection of the good (13:3). And governmental wrath upon lawlesness is the agent of God against evil doers (13:4). Therefore subjection to law is not only safe but right (13:5). And obedience ought to grow out of fear of judgment, but, above all, it ought to grow out of conscience. The fear of the law ought to be the least thing in obedience, while conscience ought to be the major principle in obedience to governmental laws. Therefore, taxes are prompted from conscience, and are for the support of officers, who in turn protect our consciences (13:6f).

In 13:8-10, Paul gives the one secret for keeping the law. Love is the fulfillment of all laws. He who loves his neighbor is not going to violate any relationship (13:8). The Christian does not need to seek a legal relationship with his neighbor. To recall all laws, in order to obey them with reference to a neighbor, would be a tedious and wearisome code of morals. The Christian's strength would be exhausted without fruit. But to love his neighbor is to obey and execute all obligations towards a neighbor. For love will not violate the law against adultery, murder, theft, and coveteousness (13:9a). And any other or all other commandments can be summed up in, "Thou shalt love thy neighbor as thyself" (13:9b). Love never works a hardship upon another, but always blesses (13:10a). Love is more than the letter of the law; it is the spirit of the law. "Love is the fulfillment of the law" (13:10b).

In 13:8-10, Paul gave the power for keeping the law, now in 13:11-14, he gives an incentive for law obedience, moral conduct, and good citizenship. This incentive is that we are about to step into eternal glories (13:11). We are nearer heaven than when we believed, and we ought to journey in the light of our home. We ought to live with reference to our eternal salvation. The rapid approach of our consummated salvation ought to heighten the moral character of our citizenship.

The glorious light of the eternal day is even now dispelling the darkness of the earthly night. Wherefore, we are to cease from the works of night and live in the light (13:12). Let Christians not walk as drowsy men stumbling in the dark, but as becomingly unto the day in which they live — the eternal day of heaven (13:13). And as Christians have been raised from the night, let them lay aside their former garments of the dark, and be clothed for the new day, by putting on the Lord Jesus Christ (13:14). The Christian is to be clothed in the righteousness of Christ (2 Cor. 5:21), and "the fine linen is the righteousness of saints" (Rev. 19:8).

XI

THE BELIEVER IN MORAL RELATIONS
14:1—15:13

I. The proposition concerning the eating of meat. 14:1-3.

    1. The weak ones are to be received. 14:1.

    2. The well grounded Christians may eat meat, but the weak ones can not. 14:2.

    3. The strong are not to despise the weak, nor are the weak to judge the strong. 14:3.

2. Every man is responsible to God rather than to the conscience of his neighbors. 14:4-12.

    1. The Christian is responsible to God alone. 14:4-6.
      (1) A man is just or guilty with God, and not in any man's judgment. 14:4.
      (2) In the evaluation of days. 14:5-6a.
      (3) In the evaluation of meats. 14:6b.

    2. We are responsible unto God alone in both life and death. 14:7-9.

    3. All shall stand before the judgment-seat. 14:10-12.
      (1) Then God will judge you for judging your brother. 14:10.
      (2) Live in the consciousness of the judgment. 14:11.
      (3) Each shall give an account of himself and not of another. 14:12.

3. The Christian should have regard for his neighbor's conscience. 14:13-23.

    1. Cease judging and, above all, cease being stumblingblocks. 14:13.

    2. Let none violate his own conscience. 14:14.

    3. Do not violate your brother's conscience. 14:15.

    4. Do not major on eating but upon righteousness, peace, and joy in the Holy Spirit. 14:16-19.

    5. Do not overthrow the Kingdom for meat. 14:20-23.
      (1) It is all right to eat meat. 14:20.
      (2) But it is wrong to cause a brother to stumble. 14:21.

(3) Do not be your own standard of conduct. 14:22.

(4) Do all things in faith, and what is not of faith is sin. 14:23.

4. In regarding a brother's conscience, we ought to follow Christ in self-sacrifice. 15:1-13.

1. The Christian ought to follow Christ in serving others instead of serving or pleasing self. 15:1-3.

2. The Christian is to have patience as did Christ. 15:4-6.

3. Be as cordial to one another as Jesus was in His receiving you. 15:7-12.

4. Paul's benediction upon all. 15:13.

In 14:1-3, Paul shows that difficulty had arisen concerning the eating of meat that had been offered to idols. The Gentiles made sacrifices to their heathen gods, and then utilized the meat in the city markets. The well grounded Christians knew that sin was not inherent in matter, and that meat as such was free from pollution. The weaker ones felt that it was sacrilegious for a Christian to eat meat that had been an offering unto an idol. Thus, Paul by taking neither side, shows the Christian attitude in such circumstances.

It will be remembered throughout this section, that the question is not what shall be our attitude towards a sin that we minimize, but what shall characterize our attitude towards a misunderstood question that is altogether moral. The question is not sin, but the possibility of being misunderstood. Perhaps some of the objecting Jews said: "We know sacrificial meat is not polluted nor polluting, but will the Gentiles understand us as we eat that which is sacred to their heathen gods?" No person can defend his sin with this Scripture, on the ground that he can do the evil with undisturbed conscience.

The weaker Christians are to be fellowshipped by the stronger (14:1). The well grounded Christian may eat meat, the weaker ones ought not to eat in violation of their consciences (14:2). There is no moral wrong in eating meat, but there is moral harm in violating conscience. The strong are not to despise the weak, nor are the weak to judge the strong (14:3).

In 14:4-12, the question arises as to what shall govern a man's conduct: the untrained consciences of neighbors or the will of God? Paul's answer is that every man is responsible to God alone rather than to the consciences of his neighbors. A man is just or guilty with God rather than in man's judgment (14:4). The neighbor's consciences will neither enhance nor condemn a man before God. God is the sole judge of man (14:4).

As men differ in their evaluation of various days and meats, "Let each man be fully assured in his own mind" (14:5). That is, let each man be sure that he is conscientious instead of contentious. It takes a lot of religion for some people to distinguish between their being conscientious and their being contrary. Let your contention be conscientious, but do not let your conscience be contentious (14:5f).

Paul then widens the realm in which we are responsible to God alone—in life or in death. "For none of us liveth to himself, and none dieth to himself. For whether we live, we live unto the Lord; or whether we die, we die unto the Lord: whether we live therefore, or die, we are the Lord's. For to this end Christ died and lived again, that he might be Lord of both the dead and the living" (14:7-9).

In 14:10-12, he pictures the judgment of God for a contradistinction from human judgment and to deduce sincerity and induce righteousness in every act of his readers. He first states that all will be judged for any wrong towards others (14:10). Here he takes the judgment out of human hands, as he says, God shall judge every man for having judged his brother (14:10). Then he urges in 14:11 that we live in the consciousness of the coming judgment, knowing that the Lord saith, "To me every knee shall bow, and every tongue shall confess to God." (14:11). Each one shall give an account of himself and not of another.

In 14:4-12, Paul discussed the Christian as responsible

to God alone rather than to the consciences of neighbors. Now in 14:13-23, he comes to the other side of the question, to say that the Christian should have regard for his neighbor's conscience. Though he is not responsible to his neighbor, yet he is responsible for him. He does not have to give an account of himself to his neighbor, but he must give an account to God for his relationship to his neighbor.

He says cease judging one another, and, above all, cease being stumblingblocks (14:13). The fact that a man is responsible to God makes him responsible for a brother. Being responsible to God alone does not license him to be a public stumblingblock. The Christian's relationship to God enhances his moral relationship to all others. Paul does not say, "Quit eating meat," but, "Let no man put a stumblingblock in his brother's way" (14:13). It is easy to locate the stumblingblock by the stumbling of the falling ones.

He urges in 14:14 that no one should violate his own conscience. Then in the next verse, he admonishes that no one violate his brother's conscience. 14:16-19 counsel that they should not major on eating and drinking, but upon righteousness. And these verses are summed up in 14:17, "For the Kingdom of God is not eating and drinking, but righteousness and peace and joy in the Holy Spirit."

In 14:20-23 Paul states that the Kingdom ought not to be overthrown for a "mess of pottage." He says that it is all right to eat meat (14:20), but that it is wrong to cause a brother to stumble (14:21). Eating meat is not wrong, but offending is wrong. And if eating meat offends, the Christian will glady sacrifice his liberty rather than offend. The Christian is at liberty to eat, but he has a higher right not to eat. Then he says, blessed is the man who is not his own standard of conduct (14:22). Too many people want their own consciences to be their standard of living. Christ is the standard for every life.

Great harm is done when one eats against his conscience (14:23). Let all conduct grow out of faith; and any conduct that grows out of any source other than faith is sin (14:23).

In 15:1-13, he advises the example of Christ in self-sacrifice as the governing principle in regarding a brother's conscience. Christ did not serve Himself, and pleasing of self was not His rule, but to do the will of the Father (15:3). Likewise, the Christian ought to serve others sacrificially rather than serving and pleasing self (15:1f). Patience is to characterize the Christian's self-sacrificing service (15:4-6). Then he urges that they be as cordial to one another as Jesus was in receiving them (15:7-12).

Paul concludes his discussion of the subject by pronouncing a gracious benediction upon his readers, which also shall be the glorious goal for the Christian conduct of all redeemed souls. "Now the God of hope fill you with all joy and peace in believing, that ye may abound in hope, in the power of the Holy Spirit" (15:13).

CONCLUSION

15:14—16:27

XII

CONCLUSION

15:14—16:27

1. *Reasons for the Epistle.* 15:14-33.

"And I myself also am persuaded of you, my brethren, that ye yourselves are full of goodness, filled with all knowledge, able also to admonish one another. But I write the more boldly unto you in some measure, as putting you again in remembrance, because of the grace that was given me of God, that I should be a minister of Christ Jesus unto the Gentiles, ministering the gospel of God, that the offering up of the Gentiles might be made acceptable, being sanctified by the Holy Spirit. I have therefore my glorying in Christ Jesus in things pertaining to God. For I will not dare to speak of any things save those which Christ wrought through me, for the obedience of the Gentiles, by word and deed, in the power of signs and wonders, in the power of the Holy Spirit; so that from Jerusalem, and round about even unto Illyricum, I have fully preached the gospel of Christ; yea, making it my aim so to preach the gospel, not where Christ was already named, that I might not build upon another man's foundation; but, as it is written,

'They shall see, to whom no tidings of him came,

And they who have not heard shall understand.'

(Isa. 52:15).

"Wherefore also I was hindered these many times from coming to you: but now, having no more any place in these regions, and having these many years a longing to come unto you, whensoever I go unto Spain (for I hope to

247

see you in my journey, and to be brought on my way thitherward by you, if first in some measure I shall have been satisfied with your company)—but now, I say, I go unto Jerusalem, ministering unto the saints. For it hath been the good pleasure of Macedonia and Achaia to make a certain contribution for the poor among the saints that are at Jerusalem. Yea, it hath been their good pleasure; and their debtors they are. For if the Gentiles have been made partakers of their spiritual things, they owe it to them also to minister unto them in carnal things. When therefore I have accomplished this, and have sealed to them this fruit, I will go on by you unto Spain. And I know that, when I come unto you, I shall come in the fulness of the blessing of Christ.

"Now I beseech you, brethren , by our Lord Jesus Christ, and the love of the Spirit, that ye strive together with me in your prayers to God for me; that I may be delivered from them that are disobedient in Judaea, and that my ministration which I have for Jerusalem may be acceptable to the saints; that I may come unto you in joy through the will of God, and together with you find rest. Now the God of peace be with you all. Amen." (15:14-33).

2. *Personal Mention.*   16:1-23

"I commend unto you Phoebe our sister, who is a servant of the church that is at Cenchreae: that ye receive her in the Lord, worthily of the saints, and that ye assist her in whatsoever matter she may have need of you: for she herself also hath been a helper of many, and of mine own self.

"Salute Priscilla and Aquila my fellow-workers in Christ Jesus, who for my life laid down their own necks, unto whom not only I give thanks, but also all the churches of the Gentiles: and salute the church that is in their house. Salute Epaenetus my beloved, who is the firstfruits of Asia unto Christ. Salute Mary, who bestowed much labor on you. Salute Andronicus and Junias, my kinsmen, and my fellow prisoners, who are of note among the apostles, who also have been in Christ before me. Salute Ampliatus my beloved in the Lord. Salute Urbanus our fellow-worker in Christ, and Stachys my beloved. Salute Apelles the approved in Christ. Salute them that are of the household of Aristobulus. Salute Herodion my kinsman. Salute them of the household of Narcissus, that are in the Lord. Salute Tryphaena and Tryphosa, who labor in the Lord. Salute Persis the beloved, who labored much in the Lord. Salute Rufus the chosen in the Lord, and his mother and mine. Salute Asyncritus, Phlegon, Hermes, Patrobas, Hermas, and the brethren that are with them. Salute Philologus and Julia, Nereus and his sister, and Olympas, and all the saints that are with them. Salute one another with a holy kiss. All the churches of Christ salute you.

"Now I beseech you brethren, mark them that are causing the divisions and occasions of stumbling, contrary to the doctrine which ye learned: and turn away from them. For they that are such serve not our Lord Christ, but their own belly; and by their smooth and fair speech they beguile the hearts of the innocent. For your obedience is come abroad unto all men. I rejoice over you: but I would have you wise unto that which is good, and simple unto that which is evil. And the God of peace shall bruise Satan under your feet shortly.

"The grace of our Lord Jesus Christ be with you."

"Timothy my fellow-worker saluteth you; and Lucius and Jason and Sosipater, my kinsmen. I, Tertius, who write the epistle, salute you in the Lord. Gaius my host, and of the whole church, saluteth you. Erastus, the treasurer of the city, saluteth you, and Quartus the brother." (16:1-23).

3. *Benediction.* 16:25-27

"Now to him that is able to establish you according to my gospel and the preaching of Jesus Christ, according to the revelation of the mystery which hath been kept in silence through times eternal, but now is manifested, and by the scriptures of the prophets, according to the commandment of the eternal God, is made known unto all the nations unto obedience of faith: to the only wise God, through Jesus Christ, to whom be the glory for ever. Amen." (16:25-27).

Printed in the United States of America